PRAISE FOR *THE AGE OF CREATIVITY*

"Wise and thoughtful, *The Age of Creativity* leads us through the landscape of imagination. The bonds of familial love, the workings of memory, the drive to create, and the process of aging are all explored with Urquhart's trademark blending of intelligence and warmth. This important work delves into the life of an artist who surveys the transformation of his work over decades and the parallel trajectory of his life. Urquhart's beautifully crafted memoir celebrates the longevity and the universality of the creative spirit alive in us all."
— Joanna Pocock, author of *Surrender: The Call of the American West*

"This is a gift of a book, an ode to late style, a daughter's devotional, a fascinating dive into art history, but above all a radical detonation of accepted notions of aging and art. Emily Urquhart is a curious and frank guide, who captures her subject with clear and perfect brushstrokes."
— Kyo Maclear, author of *Birds Art Life*

The Walrus Books

The Walrus sparks essential Canadian conversation by publishing high-quality, fact-based journalism and producing ideas-focused events across the country. The Walrus Books, a partnership between The Walrus, House of Anansi Press, and the Chawkers Foundation Writers Project, supports the creation of Canadian nonfiction books of national interest.

thewalrus.ca/books

Also by Emily Urquhart

*Beyond the Pale: Folklore, Family, and the Mystery
of Our Hidden Genes*

THE
AGE OF
CREATIVITY

Art, Memory, My Father, and Me

EMILY
URQUHART

ANANSI

Published in Canada in 2020 and the USA in 2020
by House of Anansi Press Inc.

www.houseofanansi.com

House of Anansi Press is committed to protecting our natural
environment. This book is made of material from
well-managed FSC®-certified forests, recycled materials,
and other controlled sources.

24 23 22 21 20   1 2 3 4 5

Library and Archives Canada Cataloguing in Publication

Title: The age of creativity : art, memory, my father, and me /
Emily Urquhart.
Names: Urquhart, Emily, author.
Identifiers: Canadiana (print) 20200206230 |
Canadiana (ebook) 20200206249 | ISBN 9781487005313 (softcover) |
ISBN 9781487005320 (EPUB) | ISBN 9781487005337 (Kindle)
Subjects: LCSH: Urquhart, Emily—Family. | LCSH: Urquhart, Tony. |
LCSH: Children of artists—Canada— Biography. |
LCSH: Painters—Canada—Biography. |
LCSH: Fathers and daughters—Canada—Biography. |
LCSH: Creative ability in old age. | LCGFT: Autobiographies.
Classification: LCC ND249.U76 U76 2020 | DDC 759.11—dc23

Book design: Alysia Shewchuk

*We acknowledge for their financial support of our publishing program
the Canada Council for the Arts, the Ontario Arts Council, and the
Government of Canada.*

Printed and bound in Canada

For my parents

When I am a hundred and ten, everything I do,
be it a dot or a line, will be alive.

KATSUSHIKA HOKUSAI

CONTENTS

Prologue: Still Life

I SAW THE TWO OF us framed in the mirror behind
the bar. The mirror's surface was smoky and dim,
an effect of the candlelight flickering from the tables
behind us. There were several rows of glass liquor
bottles on the counter below the mirror, as well as
a silver-lidded mason jar filled with sugar cubes, a
modest pile of white napkins, and a half-peeled lemon
in a white porcelain bowl. It was as if we'd stumbled
into a modern version of a Flemish still life, those
highly realist tableaux of abundance from the seven-
teenth century, where iridescent bunches of grapes
nestle beside oysters, quivering in their open shells,
half-poured wine sat stilled in glassware that is Godlike
and shiny, and the gem of a lemon's interior is exposed
by its uncurled peel.

"Who is that old guy in the mirror?" my father asked.
He was winking at himself, at me, at the passage of time.

I lifted my phone and captured an image of us—my father, at eighty-four, his face thinner than I'd seen it before, his beard as white as his hair, a tan cashmere scarf thrown across his shoulder, and me, at forty-one, half his age, a sweep of brown hair hanging into my eyes, a self-conscious half-smile, a string of red beads around my neck. He was looking up, and I was looking down, concentrating on taking the photograph of our reflection, adjusting my lens to include the lemon, the sugar, the white napkins, and the glass bottles, then waiting for a flicker of light to illuminate our faces.

The Dutch still lifes were a record of abundance, of wealth—*look at what we've reaped*—and of talent, but they also marked an important shift in the story of art. For the first time, there was no discernible subject at the heart of these works. There was no Greek myth, no Biblical prophecy. Instead, they were a study of shape and form, light and shadow, and of objects grouped in space. In this way, the Dutch artists took the first steps towards abstraction in art. They created antecedents to larger studies of light in impressionism, of form in cubism, of the abstract, non-figurative works that followed from the nineteenth century onwards. If I looked long enough at these still lifes, I could see my father's abstract expressionist paintings, those towering canvases that were the backdrop to my childhood.

These still lifes were not without narrative, however. There was an undercurrent of caution to the works, ever present, always a reminder that the depicted luxuries were ephemeral—no goods could bind the human spirit to earth. The *memento mori* of these banquet scenes, innocuous, beautifully uncurled, was often the lemon: a peeled fruit will begin to rot.

And now, four centuries later, here was the peeled lemon, sitting almost aglow, in the white bowl on the lip of a bartender's counter. We were living on the fringes of our time of plenty by then, holding on, grasp growing fainter. My father was struggling with his memory, and his pace had slowed, but his work—or, rather, his vocation, as he called his daily art practice—continued unabated, revealing creativity to be an act as inevitable and constant as death itself.

The image of me and my father in the mirror was a conflation of life, art, and time. It was an echo of the years we travelled Europe together, looking at art, as I wandered, learning how to see, and my father sketched or studied the work of the great artists who'd lived long before him, as he'd done since he was a young man.

In recent years, these were memory tours for my father, as he turned the album pages of postcards he'd collected from the churches, towns, museums, and pilgrimage sites he visited over six decades, ranging from the soaring turrets of a Gothic cathedral to the minute—a single white bone resting on velvet and encased in gold and glass, the relic of a long-gone saint. In these souvenirs he re-travelled the landscapes of his memory, drawing on the many tiers of his long, long life, and returned fresh-eyed and anew to his practice.

We travel together so briefly through time. We carry each other's memories forward, and this overlap makes histories, ones as grand as the story of art, or as small as a family origin tale. These series of moments gather into wisdom, growing with each year, so that in the end, there is a deep well to draw from, although always more to learn. It's impossible to know who will leave early, and who will stay late, and what might come in the final stage of a life—a swan song, or something smaller but no less important, a purpose fulfilled. As Carl Jung wrote of old age, "the afternoon of human life must also have a significance of its own and cannot be merely a pitiful appendage to life's morning." Our lifespans are elastic; our twilights are stretching. For some, the finale will be the best part of the show.

When my father and I looked into the dusky, timeless mirror above the bar, the man captured within was a craftsperson whose skills were honed, whose wellspring of talent was bolstered by nearly a century of practice, placing him at the pinnacle of his artistic life as he closed in on his eighty-fifth year. My father was but one example of the longevity of the creative spirit, alive in all of us. Who was the old man in the mirror? I had only one answer: He was my father, the artist.

The Earth Returns to Life

MY FIRST MEMORY of my father is a shimmer, a painterly abstraction of form and light. This isn't because of the fractures of memory, although these are also at play. It is because I am viewing him through water.

I was three years old and I'd been picnicking with my parents on the bank of the Source-Seine river in France. We'd driven there from Flavigny-sur-Ozerain, the small medieval village where we lived that year during my father's sabbatical, settling into the French landscape and culture that had captivated his imagination since he was in his early twenties. Now he was in his mid-forties, my mother, thirty. At our picnic spot there were tall trees, bushy with foliage, and a path that divided the woods. We'd laid out our blanket and food on a bed of soft grass near the water, and had eaten lunch. I was playing with a red rubber ball that fit perfectly into my cupped palms, and it had rolled into the riverbed, which was reedy and green, camouflaging the water beneath as if it were an extension of the meadow. I'd ambled after the ball, and while my parents finished their food, or talked, or looked into the light-dappled canopy of trees, I'd overreached, lost my balance, and fallen backwards into the river. I was beneath the surface but lying face-up so that, eyes open, I could see treetops overhead through the water, which was streaked with reeds — paint-strokes of shining green against a blue-white sky, the sun a prism of light. I'd been struck immovable by fear, terrified by the sudden silence and breathlessness of being submerged, and by the immediate shift in the appearance of the landscape. Crisp lines had been obscured by ripples; the contours of nature were now blurry and abstract. I don't remember my lungs filling with water, so I must have known instinctively to hold my breath. A man's face appeared above me, distorted, features washed clean. I saw a bearded chin, topped by a wild tuft of greying brown hair. In this alternate world, he was not recognizable as my father. Instead, I believed the man hovering overhead was Jesus.

My family wasn't religious — we'd never attended church, or spoken of God, but my father drew on spiritual places, both natural and built, in his work. These were often pilgrimage sites for religious travellers — and also for my father, who returned, often, to sketch at these holy places. Recently, along with my parents, I'd climbed the tall mountain above the holy well at Lourdes, occasionally crawling on my knees, mimicking the actions of the pilgrims as we all made our way through the Stations of the Cross. The statues were golden and life-sized, with vacant, unblinking eyes, and Jesus, a young, bearded man, was at the centre of each tableau undergoing a succession of brutalities, from condemnation to having his body nailed to the cross, with the final three scenes depicting his harrowing death and subsequent entombment.

The Stations of the Cross were my first remembered encounter with religion, and, also, with violence. I'd wept at Lourdes, rattled and filled with sorrow for what happened to the golden man at the hands of people he'd believed were his friends. The story of Jesus became etched into my consciousness, as frightening stories tend to settle into a child's grey matter, and so those scenes came to me as I lay, stilled and wide-eyed on the riverbed, believing that I was drowning. I was underwater for only a few seconds, but time was meaningless. It felt as if I'd been there all of my life.

My memory of this event is corrupted. It is a memory of a memory, a memory of a dream, a tale passed down to me from my parents, and from myself. The watery, wordless vision of my father has remained vividly intact, however, and so too has the feeling that came when the spell, and the silence, was broken, and the world around me regained clarity as my father, not Jesus, lifted me from the river and into his arms. My first memory of my father is an abstraction, a world distorted, beautifully and terribly, a swirling skyscape, a rippled impression, inspired by the spiritual landscape that had drawn him to that country, the landscape that, every day in his studio, he recreated in altered form, in ink on the page, paint on the canvas, in tall, strange sculptures. In this way, my first memory of my father is also my first memory of art.

IT WAS ON A bright day in autumn, during the period when the friends of my parents had begun to die, that my father showed me one of his early paintings, and it changed the way I understood creativity — specifically, its longevity. It was September of 2016. The leaves were still green. We were visiting the Art Gallery of Ontario. Earlier in the day, we'd been at a memorial service that was housed in an airy glass enclosure that nevertheless felt suffocating. My father, who was then eighty-two, was wearing a grey suit coat and a tan collared shirt. His neon-green glasses hung on a string around his neck. His hair and beard, trimmed neatly that day, had been white since I was a teenager. He'd been easy to spot in the crowd that had gathered after the service. He never wore black. Not a suit coat, not his shoes, not even a tie. He'd grown up in a funeral home, so he'd seen enough black. It was a family business that stretched back four generations to the founder — sunken-eyed and ghost-like, the fading image of our ancestor hung in an ornate oval frame on the dining room wall of my childhood home. My father revered and respected this part of his past, but he would never become an undertaker. He would only ever be an artist.

Once in the gallery, my father led me to a boxy room on the second floor that showcased a small collection of Canadian postwar paintings. Here, he began to circle the room, his hands clasped neatly behind his back, his neck strained forward as he leaned in to examine certain paintings. It was a personal choreography that he performed in all galleries—the way he would get as close to the art as the rules allowed, his nose nearly grazing the canvas. His own art, the sculptures, not the paintings or drawings, were meant to be touched and repositioned, changed by the whim of the viewer. It was a conundrum, as it is forbidden to rearrange art on display in public galleries and discouraged in commercial and private collections. But then, my father's work has never followed the rules. I'd witnessed him touch and move his own sculptures while passing through an art gallery, re-angling a door of one of his curio cabinets to better showcase the three-dimensional landscape within. This invariably alerted security. Years before, I'd watched with trepidation as my father rearranged one of his sculptures in a public gallery and a red-faced guard called in backup on her walkie-talkie, a garbled message I could not catch, but was probably something like, "There's an old guy fiddling with a sculpture."

This scene was no doubt familiar to her, someone leaning in too close, stray fingers, a bump from a handbag or backpack, but what she didn't know was that this old guy had been fiddling with art all his life. When she approached, he told her that he was the artist, and that it was okay. She rolled her eyes and blew air out of her puffed cheeks.

"We'll leave," I offered.

"No, you won't," she countered. "I've got an incident report to fill out."

My dad had remained in place, patiently answering the guard's questions as she completed her form, giving her his name and proffering his driver's licence for the curious spelling of our Scottish surname. He described to her the rationale behind his interactive works, that being able to reposition a sculpture created an important relationship between viewer and art, allowing for a fluid, ever-changing piece of work. In this way the gallery patron experienced the work individually and was master, to a small extent, of the form, inviting them into the process of creation, and breaking down the usual barrier that exists between the artist, their art, and the viewing public, he said. It was the opposite of traditional art, the stilled canvases and stoic sculptures that populate gallery spaces. The guard, in turn, explained that any time someone touched a piece of art there was a complex reporting system that she was forced to engage in, and that it took a long time. He said he understood that this was the gallery policy, and acknowledged that she was just doing her job. He flashed her his crowded and toothy smile. She smiled, tentatively, back at him, and I saw that she'd cracked a little, some light had gotten in. They'd reached a truce. By the end, he'd won her over.

I WANDERED TO THE BACK corner of the Canadian post-war painting show space, and was looking at a black dot on a white canvas, and, on the adjacent wall, a rich, red painting, when my father approached me and guided me to the east wall.

"Do you see any of your friends here?"

I knew what he was asking. It was a game familiar to me since childhood. Sometimes I could identify the hands behind the brushstrokes, or the sculptor's mark. I'd spent a lifetime accompanying my dad to art galleries across Europe and North America, and I'd completed my undergraduate degree in art history. No matter how I might study, however, I could never match my father's extensive internal art catalogue. No one could. Every September, for the four decades that he taught fine arts, first at the University of Western Ontario, then at the University of Waterloo, he'd challenged the new crop of undergraduate students to find an image from the art history department's slide library that he couldn't identify.

"I've never been stumped," he'd tell them.

This was not true, but it wasn't an enormous stretch, either. In forty years, it had happened only a handful of times.

I'd known the black dot painting was by Claude Tousignant, famed Montreal-based geometric abstractionist, and the red work was by Yves Gaucher, who had also lived in Montreal. However, I wasn't able to identify any of the four abstract paintings on the other side of the room. I couldn't even guess.

He walked closer to a painting in the middle.

"What about this one?"

I approached a mid-sized canvas. In it, patches of earth, frothy water, trees, and roots had all been tossed apart by some unseen natural force. Fields of muted colours seeped out from the middle and into the corners. I conceded defeat.

"I don't know it."

"You might."

My father plucked the catalogue from a nearby shelf, opened it to the page referencing the east wall, and ran his finger across the list of paintings and their makers until he came to rest on his own name.

The Earth Returns to Life. 1958. Tony Urquhart. b. 1934—.

"No death date," he said. "I'm the only one still alive."

MY FATHER WAS TWENTY-FOUR years old when he painted *The Earth Returns to Life.* He was skinny, his hair was slicked into a point above his forehead, like a cresting wave, and he had a shadowy moustache. He worked out of his childhood home in Niagara Falls, a two-storey Colonial building with multi-paned windows which was attached to the family-run funeral parlour. He lived with his parents, his maternal grandmother, and his younger brother. His granny, fierce and loyal, had repurposed part of her office sunroom on the second floor into a studio for my father. She sat at a bureau on one side, doing the funeral home's bookkeeping, and recording the bodies that turned up downriver from the falls, which she did as a pastime but which, of course, related to her work as an undertaker. My father occupied the other half of the space, painting giant, increasingly abstract canvases. When his granny wasn't in the room, my father played records, the piano concertos, arias, and operas that have carried him throughout his life. He paused his player during funeral services.

"You just knew to be quiet," he said. He'd been trained to do so since early childhood.

The smell of oil paint, unmistakably toxic and thick, couldn't have escaped the attention of the gathered mourners. (Perhaps they assumed the fumes were embalmer's fluid.) The first few notes of the organ signalled the beginning of the service, when silence was imperative. When the organ started up again it meant that the procession was leaving the building and heading towards the cemetery. After waiting for the last of the mourners to clear, my father could restart his record player and continue painting.

As my father came of age in the 1950s, North American artists began making work that didn't replicate nature but, instead, deconstructed the living world. The artwork was lifelike in its energy—the sweep of large brushstrokes, the dripping of paint—but it was not realistic, not a mirror of the known world. Instead, there was a focus on colour, movement, and shape. Collectively, the period of art was named abstract expressionism and called "America's last great spiritual movement."

By the mid-1950s, the New York art scene rivalled that of Paris, and abstract expressionists were leading the revolution. Willem de Kooning, who'd arrived in the U.S. as a young stowaway on a ship that left his native Antwerp and docked in Virginia, had produced his series of *Woman* paintings at the beginning of the decade. His abstractions hinted at portraiture that was both sacred and profane. In these paintings, the woman's body took up most of the canvas and yet she was difficult to decipher, obscured by layers of cross-hatched lines and aggressive paint-strokes. In *Woman I*, which took several years to paint, you can make out the woman's bulging eyes and elongated teeth, but where her body begins and ends is difficult to tell. She is both zombie-like and beguiling, a Madonna and a whore. Meanwhile, de Kooning's contemporary, Jackson Pollock, had extended the physicality of art to include the movements of his entire body as he flicked and dripped paint across his giant canvases, gracefully, brashly, not a brushstroke in sight, his efforts inspiring the term "action painting." These art stars were household names, celebrities even. Their influence stretched north of the border and it was the first time that being an artist was seen as a potential career—outside of being a war artist or a member of the Group of Seven, whose landscapes had, earlier that century, built the foundation for what was historically considered Canadian art.

My father, young, focused, and talented, was among the converts to abstract expressionism, and the influence of the New York artists on his work was profound.

My grandfather was an American expatriate, and the border had always been fluid for my father's family. (My great-grandmother's morning chore was to ride her tricycle across the suspension bridge between the two countries to pick up a loaf of bread for breakfast.) My father was twenty-one when he began crossing the border every day to attend the Albright Art School in Buffalo, the closest art school to his home in Niagara Falls. The school was closely aligned with the Albright Art Gallery, now called the Albright-Knox, an early supporter of abstract expressionism, with deep collections of de Kooning, Pollock, and colour field painter Mark Rothko, whose translucent blocks of paint vibrated on giant canvases but were suggestive of nothing—not landscape, not portrait, just a symbiosis of colours.

The first group show of abstract works in Toronto happened in 1954. The artists in the group called themselves Painters Eleven, and were banded together by their dedication to abstract art, not necessarily their styles, which ranged from geometric patterning to seemingly haphazard slashes of paint diagonally across a canvas. Three years after the group formed, my father had his first one-man show, at age twenty-two. At the onset of his twenties he'd been signed by renowned Toronto art dealer Av Isaacs, who recognized my father's potential when he was still a student. The Isaacs Gallery roster grew to include some of the most important Canadian artists of the late twentieth century, including Michael Snow, William Kurelek, and Joyce Wieland. When my father graduated from art school two years after his first show, his work was selling across the country. Critics called him a "boy wonder," and his career attracted the intense fascination and fawning awe spurred by young genius. Owning one of his paintings was a status symbol among the Niagara Falls elite. *The Earth Returns to Life* left his sunroom studio tucked under the arm of the local power station owner, my father told me as we stood before his early painting.

"He was a toff," my dad said.

I didn't always understand the words in my father's vocabulary, which was rooted in the beginning of the last century. He still called the fridge an "ice box."

"What's a toff?"

"A monied man."

"How could you tell?"

"He wore a camel's-hair coat."

Fifty years later the piece turned up at auction, where Toronto-based media magnate David Thomson purchased it, then donated it to the Art Gallery of Ontario along with a swath of his family's considerable collection of Canadian art.

"This is yours?" I said, leaning into the painting, my hands clasped behind my back, adopting my father's art-viewing stance. On closer inspection, I saw how the atmospheric background and otherworldly organic matter of the landscape in oil hinted at my father's later and better-known abstract expressionist works. His large-scale paintings from the 1960s and the 1980s were similarly earth-toned but more abstract, and inspired by the European countryside. (From 1963 to 1980, he worked exclusively in sculpture.) Spooky shapes were often foregrounded by a hovering darkness. I think of the haystack painting that loomed over the sideboard (in itself a work of art, carved by my undertaker ancestors) in my childhood home. The haystack, the bulbous shape that takes up most of the 4-by-3-foot canvas, is ominous, dark—but, on closer inspection, laced with many colours, the oil paint complex, layered, with surprising spots of baby blue and dusky rose. On the left are ambiguous trees in a landscape that is seemingly rushing off the canvas in a sort of waterfall. On the right, some dark shape hovers, threatening to snuff out everything in its path under a slate-grey sky.

Paintings like these were the products of uneasy times: Canada was on the fringes of the Cold War, and my father's art was imbued with nuclear threat. That changed when he entered his sixties. In the late 1990s and early 2000s, freed from those earlier anxieties, vibrant, almost supernatural colours appeared on his canvases in a series of self-portraits called *My Garden*. In one, a palm tree snakes up the middle of a Florida-inspired landscape, the background a lime-green sky. On the left, there is a small black-and-white cut-out photograph of my father as a toddler in his sandbox. On the right, his American grandparents, the year before his grandfather died. There is a sharp crease in his grandfather's trousers and his grandmother wears a hat. They are staid and sophisticated, a strange contrast to the painting's neon-light aesthetic. The tension of his earlier work remains, but the mood has lifted. Where there had been foreboding, there is now intrigue. Something spiritual glows on the horizon.

My father's work is a language I've learned since birth. Often, in reading his images I could give the provenance, the general timeframe, and the geographic location of what had inspired the piece—a French cemetery in the seventies, the white willows on the banks of the pond that surrounded my childhood home in the eighties, the germinating ruin of an Irish famine cottage in the nineties—because often the subject matter mirrored where he had lived and travelled in his various life stages.

And yet, there in the gallery, I hadn't been able to identify *The Earth Returns to Life* as my father's work, nor could I guess what geography might have acted as inspiration. I'd been stumped.

"It's overly figurative," he said. "The trees are too much themselves, too literal." He felt that it hadn't undergone a necessary transformation into abstraction. He quarrelled with the value, a principal element of art which refers to the darkness or lightness of colour and how these opposing qualities are placed in accordance with one another to create depth and contrast, and to balance the work.

"Stand back and squint," he said.

I stood, crinkled my eyes until my vision blurred, and noticed how the darker hues drew my line of vision into the bottom-left corner of the painting, outweighing the lighter regions of the right upper half.

"It's immature," he concluded, critiquing the work as if it had been painted by one of his students, rather than his former self.

THERE WERE ALMOST SIXTY years between *The Earth Returns to Life* and that day in the gallery. It was made before my father's inaugural trip to Europe, with his first wife, where he underwent what can only be described as an aesthetic conversion, brought about after seeing the Roman Catholic churches—flickering candles, the solemnity of High Mass, the gilded and the golden, the frescoes—as well as the Paleolithic cave paintings, and, the crowning event, master draughtsman Goya's drawings in the Museo del Prado archives during a jaunt to Madrid. He'd travelled there by ocean liner using funds from his first successful arts grant, feeling validated by his peers who'd sat on the jury. It was the first time he'd left North America, although he'd studied European art extensively, and so this spiritual commingling—holding Goya's work in his hands, bringing it close enough to see each mark that made up the composition as a whole—established his succession in a long line of artists who'd made exactly this kind of pilgrimage before him. He had placed himself in the world, cementing his identity as an artist, and also his life's purpose.

Eight years later, while he and his wife were stationed in Dublin for the summer with a cacophony of small children—my half-siblings—my father took a short trip to Bavaria and saw the pilgrimage churches and their triptychs and diptychs. He returned home and, using a sabre saw, he pried apart the sculptures he'd created before he'd left. He then added doors, creating neatly designed cupboards that opened to reveal organic sceneries, otherworldly, vaguely mirroring our own geographies. These are the sculptures he gleefully repositioned in galleries, raising the ire of security guards.

"Once I got them opening and closing it was like you were doing a painting and you could put a red dot there and a green area there but then you could change them and then the red might be grey and so in other words, a three-dimensional painting is what they really were," he told me. "You could move colours and textures and stuff around by adjusting the doors, and that made it way more complex and a lot more fun than just a flat painting."

He called them, simply, "boxes," although, as Joan Vastokas noted in her introduction to an exhibition catalogue of my father's work, they've been interpreted variously as symbolic landscapes, as microcosmic models of the universe, and as shrines, "metaphorical coffins, reliquaries, and grave houses." It was his sculptures that he'd become known for—their strangeness, their singularity. Spooky, deranged, whimsical, there was simply nothing else like them. The most recent box, finished the month before we visited the AGO that September, had hinged doors that were speckled with tiny pebbles from Middle Cove Beach that we'd gathered together when I lived in

Newfoundland. Inside, antique keys hung like bats in the crevices of a cave. That first movable box, created in the late sixties, with doors that swung open on hinges to reveal a world within, had lit a fire. He didn't return to painting on canvas until 1980, when I was a toddler and we lived in France for the year. Shipping costs were high. It was cheaper to ship several paintings home in a crate than several sculptures, and my father always liked a deal.

Now, in his eighties, my father was a composite of the young artist in a glass studio, painting opposite his granny while she carefully tallied the tolls of the dead, and the artist father of four small children, returning to Europe for the seventh time, knowing, as he hadn't known on that first voyage, to order wine rather than milk to drink with dinner—remembering the utter bafflement of the French waiter on the MS *Hanseatic*. He was the midlife father of a new small child—with his second wife, my mother—returning like a pilgrim to holy sites across France, to the Stations of the Cross, to Rocamadour, stopping to picnic on the banks of the Source-Seine and fishing his toddler out of the waters after she'd fallen in. He was the artist whose canvases grew to a dizzying size in the 1980s, giant paintings of open graves that would mark some of his best work, at least in his opinion. He was the artist in his seventies, visiting the Museum of Modern Art to see the drawing show in which his work was placed alongside that of his hero, Paul Cézanne. And he was his present self, still hard at work, still acquiring new skills.

Perhaps the best example of his new vision was *Strong Box I* (2013), the first of a recent series. Seven years ago, when he was seventy-nine, my dad visited me in Victoria, British Columbia, where I lived for a time. In the past, rain or shine, he would leave the house to ramble, perhaps discovering a grouping of oddly pollarded trees or some vegetation germinating on a tombstone to sketch. On this trip, though, he remained in the living room. There, he spent several dark winter days drawing a battered First World War chest that we'd inherited from my husband's family and used as a coffee table. I was surprised by his interest in the trunk, but even more so by his reluctance to leave the house and explore the outdoors, which had long been his muse. Months later, when I visited my parents in Ontario, the trunk was there, immortalized in an oil painting hanging above the fireplace. The trunk's worn brown patches were converted into rose, fuchsia, and vibrant blues, my living room eclipsed by a fiery-red background. And a fluorescent pink was at its centre. The trunk was still familiar, as was my father's style, but both appeared to be transformed.

The painting showed a central peach-hued rectangle bracketed by a pinkish red so intense it seemed back-lit. The repeated rectangular shapes were ambiguous, suggesting a cage or a sequence of rooms—familiar territory for my dad, as was the marbleized effect of the blended background colours and the mottled balls of organic matter that clung to the four corners of the painting's sharp, straight lines. But the colours—that pink!—were new, and they were electric. Just shy of his eightieth birthday, he'd imagined and executed something novel.

"I am still learning"—*Aun aprendo*—wrote an eighty-year-old Francisco Goya above a black-crayon drawing of a formidable old man, wild-haired and defiant, propped on two walking sticks. And he was, as lithography had recently been invented and Goya was an early adopter of this new technology near the end of his life. Not unlike contemporary artist David Hockney, who, at seventy-six, *Wired* magazine called "the world's foremost iPad painter," switching to this new medium after spending a lifetime using oil paint on canvas. And so, too, my father tried new techniques, colours, and tools as he surpassed his eighth decade and continued working, steadily, every day, at his art. So when he looked into his past—not unkindly, but with a critical lens—he saw what was yet to come and, because of this, *The Earth Returns to Life*, the abstract landscape painting that we were looking at was good, but undeveloped; or, perhaps more apt, it was, as he had been then, immature, not yet formed.

DESPITE SPENDING MOST OF my childhood drawing, I didn't grow up to become an artist. I studied art history instead. I loved art, but I loved the artists more. It was their stories that I burned for. In an oral presentation on Michelangelo's sculptures during the third year of my art history degree, I mused over the artist's romantic life. I speculated that he was in love with his sculptures, a *Pygmalion* analysis. Also, his finest sculptures were of men, so I was curious about his sexuality. I'd chosen slides from the art history library to illustrate my thesis, including the muscular twist of the *Rebellious Slave*, and the smooth-bodied, hedonistic and confident *Bacchus*, and, of course, *David*, with his youthful defiance, his tousled hair, and the details of his body so fine you could see his veins through his skin. He was beautiful, heartbreakingly so. How could the sculptor not have loved him? The lights were dimmed, my professor stood behind the slide projector so that her eyes were obscured by the machine's bright lights but I could see her mouth, which had tightened into a firm line.

"I don't think so," she said, signalling the end of my presentation. "More interpretation of the work, less speculation on the artist's personal life, please."

We were meant to be post-artist at the close of the twentieth century, instructed to understand the work as its own text, as standing apart from its maker. For a time, I complied. The artwork drew me in, and it fed me, but this method of understanding art left me hungry for more of the artist—unsated.

Over the winter of 2017 I read the biographies of great artists from back to front, sometimes beginning with the final chapters. It was a road map, of sorts, a necessary outline for an emptiness that existed in art and literature surrounding old age. As writer and editor Diana Athill, approaching ninety, wrote, "There is not much on record about falling away." Author Roger Angell, writing at ninety, said old age could feel like blankness, invisibility. He would speak at a dinner party and hear silence in return. "Hello? Didn't I just say something?" he mused. "Have I left the room?"

Reading their lives backwards, I experienced the deaths of Cézanne, Renoir, Monet, Krasner, Neel, O'Keeffe, and Turner all in one season, because the artist always died in the final pages. (The biographer has the good fortune of knowing how she will tie her writing project together.) Cézanne collapsed during a rainstorm while live-painting outdoors, *sur le motif*, lying unconscious for hours before being carried home on a laundry cart. He rallied, occasionally, over the next few days, finishing a portrait, adding some small brushes of colour to a painting near his bed — *Still Life with Carafe, Bottle, and Fruit* — and died in early morning.

Turner asked to see the sun, one last time, as he lay dying under an overcast sky. He was rewarded on the morning of his death when the sun broke through the clouds and briefly illuminated his room. He died before noon. He communicated from the afterlife in the body of a teenaged medium, the daughter of an ironworks foreman. She embodied the hunched creep of his later years, his furrowed brow. She enacted the motion of his long brushstrokes as she mimed the act of washing-in a canvas, readying it for a new painting, and she mimicked his technique of using a cloth to soften the colours on the canvas — blurring the painted weather and industrial steam. In doing this, she gave away the artistic secrets of Turner's later career.

In her twenties, suffering from depression, twentieth-century American artist Alice Neel tried repeatedly to kill herself—tied a stocking around her neck, put her head in a gas oven—but she lived to eighty-four and died of cancer, surrounded by her family in the New York City apartment that doubled as her studio.

Renoir was bedridden, and went into pulmonary arrest, hours after asking for a pencil with which to sketch a nearby vase. His gathered family couldn't find one, according to a letter written by his son, Jean. But how hard did they try? I wondered. Surely a pencil could be proffered without much trouble in the house of a dying artist. Of course, I imagined the Loyalist home in Colborne, Ontario, where my parents lived, in place of Les Colletes, Renoir's estate in Cagnes-sur-Mer, substituting familiar territory, my known life, as one does when reading the stories of others.

As each artist approached the end, the urge to create did not wane. It may have grown faint, necessarily, but the impulse to make art remained. They rose from their deathbeds to paint, asked for their tools in delirium. People who loved them bent low over their prone bodies, whispering of success, assuring them that people were still looking at the art they'd created over their lifetimes. Even Turner, unable to paint, still yearned for the light that shone through his late, great works.

WE TEND NOT TO associate aging with creative bursts. Historically, critics saw advancements by elderly artists as peculiar. According to twentieth-century art histor-ian Kenneth Clark, the work of older artists conveyed a feeling of "transcendental pessimism," best illus-trated in the weary, lined eyes and pouched cheeks of Rembrandt's late self-portraits. Claude Monet's contem-poraries decried his *Water Lilies* series as a symptom of cataracts and advanced age. The paintings were dismissed as "the work of an old man" in *Comoedia*, France's most important daily arts journal at the time. Fellow painter André Lhote described them as "artis-tic suicide." In J. M. W. Turner's final two decades, as he painted the weather, both natural and man-made, in his increasingly abstract landscapes, he found him-self brutalized by peers — a kind of aesthetic elder abuse. Turner was "without hope," wrote John Ruskin. Another, less tactful, critic said that Turner's late work was the product of "senile decrepitude."

"Now it's recognized that there was not a falling off of creative powers, but that their creative powers have changed," says Ross King, author of *Mad Enchantment: Claude Monet and the Painting of the Water Lilies.* "They were deliberately working in different ways." One brushstroke from Monet — a silhouette of a petal at dusk — holds all the shadow, richness, and texture of a life as a painter. But this is something that people often overlook. Today, it's doubtful that most gallery patrons know that Monet was in his seventies when he created the most famous paintings in his *Water Lilies* series. Turner's late creations are now widely recognized as works of incomparable brilliance. The same could be said of art from Cézanne, Titian, Michelangelo, and Rembrandt.

Lately, well-wishers had been describing my father's continued art practice as "remarkable." I sensed that his longevity and work ethic delighted them, the idea of the old artist at his easel, but I also intuited a deeper emotional response—that they were surprised by his continued creativity, and that "remarkable" was code for peculiar, or strange. As we stood before my father's early painting *The Earth Returns to Life* considering the progress of time, I wondered when and why our society had been conditioned to see creativity and aging as antagonistic. My father had always been an outlier in his talent and in his unswerving, dogged focus on art; still, in the lastingness of his creativity, he might be just like everyone else.

THERE IS A TERM, "successful aging," which has come to define a certain type of senior, one who accomplishes astonishing tasks in the final gasp of their life. These are people like the 96-year-old who ran the New York City Marathon, or the 101-year-old who released her first collection of poems. It began as a movement to counter ageism—See what we can accomplish! At any age!— but celebrating the exceptional suggests that the regular human narrative is somehow a failure. The privilege of growing old can be as much luck as circumstance. A marginalized childhood, malnutrition, stress—all can shape the later years of life. There is also the simple, bewildering fact that some bodies are able to deal with hardships and tragedies better than others. In old age there are many roads diverging, with no real control over which path anyone might end up on.

There are exciting new thoughts on the story of being old, but we're all fallible to age. It isn't something to overcome, rage against, and win over. A study of senior artists in Canada found that 73 percent, or 29,000, of the 40,000 artists polled were at a moderate or high health risk. Even the seemingly impermeable older artists featured in art history textbooks faced the realities of aging. Monet suffered from cataracts; Renoir, from painful arthritis; Degas had been blind near the end; and Lee Krasner, who'd waited all her career to see her work celebrated at the Museum of Modern Art, died unexpectedly, in her seventies, before her one-woman show was mounted. She knew it was happening, her biographer wrote. Whether this was enough, we can't know. And then there was Saloua Choucair, the Lebanese artist whose fame came in her eighties and nineties and who was alive but too deep into dementia to witness her soaring late success.

Each of these artists struggled in some way, as we all do or will, with the progress of time. And yet, Renoir found new ways to hold his brush in the tight grip of his folded hands, and Monet saw through his cataracts—or maybe he painted from memory, or based on light—but, in the end, who better than an artist to innovate through struggle? Krasner painted until she couldn't anymore, and after that, she spent time in the company of her works, communing with her creativity in a new way. In an essay by Patricia Utermohlen on her late husband's final works, she wrote that William Utermohlen's self-portraits—arresting portrayals of his descent into dementia—were a way of addressing his fears and exploring his altered self, and this necessitated a new form, new tools, even a new style. "The great talent remains," she wrote. "But the method changes."

At eighty-five, Georgia O'Keeffe's eyesight began to dim and she was unable to continue painting. Her last unassisted oil painting, *The Beyond*, was completed in 1972, and was described by her biographer Hunter Drohojowska-Philp as "Portentous and tragic... O'Keeffe's view of her immediate future."

The Beyond's foreground is dark and finite, but the horizon line and the azure sky are infinite and promising. It is light-filled, limitless. Or maybe there is no message within this work, just our competing interpretations, our need to see something past the canvas, on the horizon, so mysteriously and beautifully captured by O'Keeffe's hand. It is darker than her similar reductionist paintings of the previous decade, but rich in its darkness and hints at its artistic precursors. Did O'Keeffe know this was her final unassisted painting? Struggling with her vision, she likely knew some change was afoot. But do we ever really know when we do anything for the last time?

I no longer sing lullabies to my daughter, and neither of us remembers when we stopped the ritual. Grasping back into my memory I'm at a loss to find the end point, the finale of that important life stage. Why did I stop? The answer, of course, is that life is progress. What I know is that we began reading novels together before bed, every night, no matter how late it was, no matter where we were. It was an extension of the earlier time, and it was equally precious. O'Keeffe moved from painting to sculpture—giving us works like *Abstraction*, a twelve-foot structure of clean lines and fiddlehead curves. In a photograph by Bruce Weber taken in 1984, the artist poses with her sculpture. She wears a broad-brimmed hat that circles her head like a dark halo. She is old, her skin papery and thin, and the way she holds her body is both angular and austere. She leans on a curve of her sculpture, a long, elegant hand laid purposefully across her lap. Limitation, necessarily, inspires. Psychologist Robert Kastenbaum, whose scholarly work on death and dying redefined what we know about this stage of life, has written that creativity "may be the aging individual's most profound response to the limits and uncertainties of existence." Facing resistance—a stone wall, an impassable rush of water, a jagged-edged cliff—it is human nature to invent new pathways: a tunnel, a boat, a bridge. The most creative among us find their way, as O'Keeffe found hers.

We interpret the artist by looking at her work, but our inferences are more a mirror of ourselves. *The Beyond* was construed by many as meaningful for its place in the artist's oeuvre, its title a tragic nod to her end. But this is ageist and ableist, because O'Keeffe didn't stop there. After switching mediums, she continued creating work for another fourteen years. Maybe the title hinted at a new frontier; one waiting to be conquered and mastered, just past the dark horizon.

King and Queen

THERE WERE MANY ROOMS in my childhood home on William Street in the city of Waterloo, but only two remain etched in my memory — my father's studio, and the kitchen. It was the 1980s and most of the home had wall-to-wall green shag carpeting, but the kitchen floor was covered in yellow linoleum, a faux-tile design of flowers encased in boxes. There was a small breakfast alcove with a bank of windows that faced south. In it sat our round kitchen table, crowded with half-grown children, shoulders and knees bumping, the dog nosing the floor beneath my high chair — which sat in the corner, facing the windows, until I was old enough to sit on one of the brightly coloured chairs with the other children. On weekdays, these were my older half-sisters, Allyson and Robin. Allyson, the oldest, nearing adulthood, had permed blonde hair, and wore tight jeans and green eyeshadow. She was obsessively entangled with her boyfriend, and, also, with gymnastics. Robin, the second oldest, was a blue-eyed brunette with a scattering of freckles across her nose. Curious, bright, and dyslexic, she'd learned to read as a teenager when my mother met her and discovered she was illiterate. Before that, remarkably, she'd passed through life with her disability undetected. Most nights Robin left early for her shift as a ticket collector at the downtown movie theatre, a few blocks from our house. Allyson would leave shortly afterwards for gymnastics practice, and then, later, to see her boyfriend. My two older half-brothers, Marsh and Aidan, both younger teens, arrived from London, where they lived with their mother, on Friday nights to spend the weekend. Marsh, the older of the two, was dark-haired like his mother and wore glasses. He'd lisped as a younger child, and was a quiet teen, watchful and nervous, but had a staccato yipping laugh when something surprised him. He trusted no one and was protective of his family, particularly of Aidan and, later, of me. He seemed more adult than peer, while in Aidan, who was only nine years older than me, I spied the possibility of a playmate. My affection for him was suffocating, though, so he mostly dodged my attention in favour of our older siblings. Aidan had a toothy smile like our father, and a bowl cut that rested just above his big brown eyes. He was alert, like an animal, and the kind of handsome child older ladies fussed over.

The boys were gone again by Sunday afternoons. The rotating schedules worked because there wasn't enough room at our kitchen table, or even available chairs, for everyone to sit down all at once. My mother, Jane, who orchestrated the feeding of this rotation of schedules and appetites, had no designated seat at the table, and often there was no room for her at all. She spent mealtimes in the adjacent kitchen, side-stepping from sink to stove to fridge and back again in a choreography that would whisk her through her mid-twenties and into her early thirties.

My mother had been widowed and childless when she met my father at one of his art openings. It was a group show at the Kitchener-Waterloo Art Gallery. The exhibition poster now hangs on my kitchen wall. My mother hadn't wanted to go. She hadn't wanted to go anywhere, ever again, since her young husband, Paul Keele, an artist, was killed in a car accident nearly a year before. A friend insisted she attend the opening, saying that she needed to get out of the house, and she'd relented. That night she met my father. There were obvious challenges—he was a divorcee with four children, two of whom lived with him, and he was fifteen years her senior. It's impossible to test this theory, but my mother has always insisted that she was still in shock when they met, which is why she walked into this complicated family arrangement. But, recently, she admitted it was also partly that my father was an undertaker's son. He'd spoken of her deceased husband with ease. He'd asked about Paul's art, but also inquired if the embalmer had done a good job and wondered what kind of casket she'd chosen to house his body. After they met, my father took my mother to Europe, impressing her with his vast knowledge of European art as they toured art galleries and museums. They'd also visited a number of French cemeteries so that my father could sketch tombstones, obelisks, mausoleums.

"Most people wouldn't even bring up Paul's name, never mind the fact that he was dead, and here was this guy who was talking all about it and taking me to graveyards all the time and showing me ossuaries filled with human bones. And yet it was completely life-enhancing," my mother told me. "It brought me back to life."

Back home, my father introduced my mother, still grieving and low, to a milieu of artists and writers, people my mother was awed by but with whom she quickly found she could keep pace — in conversation, in thought, and in ideology — and in this dawned a possibility that maybe she might have something to say that was worthwhile, too.

During the years when my mother had no seat at the kitchen table, she was also writing, and had published a few poems in literary magazines. She'd go on to write several books of poetry, a collection of short stories, and many novels. Her career as an author would be large and successful. But back when she was in her twenties, she was still learning her craft, toiling only when she could, when everyone left for the day — my father to teach at the university, my sisters to high school. She wrote in the silence of these afternoons, when I was a baby and still napping, and later, in the time between drop-off and pick-up when I too went to school. In these spaces of quiet and solitude, the round table was empty of children, of dishes and chaos and half-eaten food, and all the rainbow-coloured chairs were free. She could sit, and write, wherever she liked.

WHEN HE WASN'T TEACHING, my father worked out of a studio in the basement. The space was cave-like, musty, and often damp. It was also poorly ventilated. Oil paint fumes commingled with the smell of turpentine, the chemical solvent my father used to wash paint colours from his skin. The stairs that led from the first floor down to the basement were steep and had no railing. Because of the rickety stairs and the toxic fumes, and also my age—we lived in this house until I was seven—I was forbidden from accompanying my father into his studio while he worked.

This rule did not extend to my brothers when they visited on weekends. In the morning they slipped through the door off the kitchen and disappeared into the basement for most of the day, surfacing only for food and sleep. My sisters lived with us full-time, but they were in their late teens and both unbothered and uninterested in the underground life of our father and brothers.

The studio was a modest-sized room, which sat under an extension at the front of the house and was accessed by a doorway that led from a smaller room at the foot of the stairs. It had no natural light, so my father used standing spotlight lamps. Searing and focused, they illuminated his towering canvases, which were, during that period, often abstractions of open graves. He called them his *Threshold* series. These were painterly in execution and yet also grotesque, seeming to germinate in their decrepitude. He named the largest *King and Queen* and the second largest *King and Queen II*.

King and Queen was a deep-scarlet four-panelled painting that stood ten feet tall. The two bottom panels were of open graves, which were rectangular in shape and human-sized. They appeared three-dimensional and, because the painting stood upright, as if they were hallways leading deep into the earth, doors to the underworld. A painted wreath of dried flowers and pieces of bone circled each top panel—these were the monarchs' crowns. When finished, the four panels were separately shrouded in plastic and the two parts stood like sentries on either side of the entrance to the studio.

At nine feet, *King and Queen II* was slightly smaller, and also more three-dimensional, approaching sculpture. My father had ripped into the canvas and lined the tear with black velvet to create a spatial *trompe l'oeil*, as if now, instead of tunnelling into the earth, the viewer was gazing into nothing, or maybe everything, the whole universe a black hole.

During those years, my father's paintings were nearly all as large as the *King and Queen* works. When he finished a painting, he wrapped it in thick plastic, as he'd done with *King and Queen*, and stacked it against the stairs to the main floor. This area became a resting place for finished pieces that were ready to be packed into a rented truck and driven the hour or so to Toronto where my father would show and, he hoped, sell them.

When I was left unattended, and if I stayed quiet, I was sometimes able to pass through the basement door unnoticed. I could creep halfway down the stairs and sit hidden behind the large paintings propped there. In this way I could peer over the lip of the frame and through the studio entrance to watch my two brothers work alongside our dad. Marsh's dark hair hung into the frames of his glasses when he bent over his work. He was a draughtsman, careful and exacting in his execution. Realistic, unflinching, he caught life in his hands. His prints were exquisite, his lines delicate — a human face in laughter, a duo of apples on a sill. Aidan buzzed while he worked, his synapses firing. It was always colour for him, colour and ideas. A lightning-bolt artist, his thoughts came quickly. Bizarre political slogans floated through his paintings, which were deceptively bright, and almost decorative. In one, a cartoonish young man stared directly at the viewer, blood splattered across his face. A banner running behind him read: *You never know!*

Then there was my father, standing at his palette mixing oil paints and wearing his royal-blue overcoat, buttoned up the front to protect his clothes. The coat was decorated in smears of paint. Years of brushes and fingers had been wiped clean on its breast and cuffs. It would eventually become stiff and cracked and need replacing, and the process would start anew.

The high-pitched wail of the table saw filled the space intermittently — wood being cut and shaped into frames for canvases or for the bases of my dad's sculptures. The saw was another reason I was barred from the studio. My mother felt it was too dangerous and that I would likely sever my fingers by running my hand along the spinning steel blade. The saw's noise competed with Chopin, Haydn, Rachmaninoff, piano concertos that provided a frenzied soundtrack, as if the studio and the characters within it were in a play or a film. The spotlights illuminated the three of them like actors on a set pretending to be artists, and when I was a young child, the only viewer of this theatre and seated behind the fourth wall, they were equally impenetrable. It was a magic, subterranean world, a place where boys toiled at their craft alongside an old master surrounded by the open graves of unnamed royalty, but it was not a place for a little girl.

WE SEE THE WORLD first through the dynamics of our family and the constellation of people they bring into our orbit. I saw men who were artists and women who were mothers, some with grown children, some with younger children, but in my earliest years, I do not remember women visual artists. I have memories of being taken to art shows of work by men. I remember hoovering up the crackers and olives on the buffet table and feeling oblivious and small in the chatter of the adult crowd. I remember the walls of homes we visited, decorated with the art of the owner—nearly always a man—and I can, in some cases, bring to mind their studios: an unused guest room, an outbuilding in the country, or, as in my father's friend Hugh Mackenzie's case, under the peaked top-floor ceiling of the narrow townhome in Toronto that he shared with his wife, Dot Mackenzie.

Dot was a small, bright-eyed woman who wore her grey-black hair twisted into a bun on the top of her head. She was apple-cheeked and open-faced and had the voice of a determined smoker, which was both gravelly and sophisticated. I remember her petite frame in flowing dresses threaded with silver, sleeveless in summer, worn over turtlenecks in winter. Once, when she came to stay at my parents' home in Stratford while taking a week-long course on Shakespearean drama, I saw her eat half a banana and save the rest for later. I was astonished that this tiny morsel of food had sated her.

After Dot died in her mid-eighties, as Hugh and their children sifted through her belongings, they discovered a portrait she'd painted of me when I was seven, and Hugh gave it to me. The photograph she'd worked from was tucked into the folds at the back of the canvas. There was a smudge of white paint on the image, and a faint splatter of peach (my skin colour, I guessed) across the back. These traces of paint, along with the small pinprick from a thumbtack, must have been remnants of where she'd pinned it while painting. And yet, as I examined the marks she'd left on the photograph, I wasn't able to envision Dot's studio.

I called my mother, hoping she might help to jog my memory.

"Did Dot have a studio in the house on Macpherson?" I asked, holding the photograph in my hand. Dot had been dead for several years by then.

"Sure, she had a studio," my mother said. "It was in a room on the second floor."

"I don't remember that," I said.

"We've always had her work hanging in our house," my mother said, and she described two watercolours, one of trees on a hill at dusk and the second of lemons in a bowl, a pale, delicate still life that I could immediately call to mind. I also remembered Dot painting my portrait—but I realized now that I hadn't understood that art was her vocation.

"Honestly, I don't think I knew she was an artist."

"She was," my mother said, her voice firm. "Of course she was."

AT OUR FAMILY HOME in Waterloo, undeterred by the rules of who could and who could not enter my father's workspace, I continued to creep down the stairs to the basement studio. Once, sitting behind a large-scale canvas, I grasped the lip of the frame to pull myself up and get a better look, forgetting that it was a painting, not a railing. The painting tipped forward, but I didn't let go. I fell with it, slowly, horrifyingly. How many feet? Nine, maybe ten? I can feel the sensation of falling even now, and the sense of dread. I was sure I'd be punished, probably spanked. All of the children knew that ruining our father's art was an unforgivable offence.

I can bring the painting to mind—though only faintly now—and it appears to be several works from my father's *Threshold* series fused into one. What I remember is that it was a large, hunter-green abstraction and that it was an open grave. I remember my father and brothers rushing from the studio to my side, standing above me as I lay on the floor. I remember how our deranged family dog had run down the stairs, the tags on his collar jingling, and how my mother and sisters followed. The memory of my fall ends here. After this, it goes dark.

IT WAS A MID-AFTERNOON in March, six months after I'd visited the Art Gallery of Ontario in Toronto with my father, and I was visiting my parents at their home in Colborne, a small town about an hour east of the city. They lived in a sprawling house that had belonged to my maternal grandparents. I'd driven there the previous day along with my husband, Andrew, our two children, who were then aged six and two, and our dog, from our home in Kitchener. After ten years away, I'd recently moved back to the region where I'd grown up, when Andrew, who is a scientist, was offered a job as a professor at the University of Waterloo, the institution that had employed my father for most of his career.

My daughter was at my parents' kitchen table, drawing while listening to an audiobook, and my son was napping in an upstairs bedroom. I found my father sitting at his piano, sheet music, yellowed with age, open in front of him. He was playing the first notes of Bach's "Jesu, Joy of Man's Desiring." It was familiar to me from childhood, when he'd practised it on the baby grand that once sat below my bedroom, decades and houses ago. Today, in his early eighties, he was playing on a small upright piano in his drawing room—not the old-fashioned way of saying "living room," but, literally, the room where he draws. It was a rare moment alone with my father and marked the first of many conversations we'd have, over the next two years, about life and art.

He was wearing a soft brown cable-knit cardigan over a collared shirt and grey pants. It was a kind of uniform. He wore a variation of this outfit every day. This was his drawing room, and he didn't need his blue painting overcoat here. His studio, for the first time, had been severed: organized into wet and dry. A small back room served as his painting studio, but he used it less and less. He complained that it was cold in winter, stifling in summer, and also somewhat cramped. The drawing room was temperate, comfortable, and had good light. It was large enough to house his record collection and his extensive library of art catalogues, in shelves that lined three of the four walls. He spent his time there sketching and painting with watercolours and acrylics, creating works on paper rather than making oil paintings or sculptures. In the past few years, this room had become his world.

My father's glasses were perched on the edge of his nose as he read the sheet music. He was focused, engulfed by the notes he was playing and oblivious to his surroundings. I touched his shoulder gently to let him know I was there. He stopped playing, took his glasses from his nose, turned, and smiled. In the silence, I heard the clock ticking above our heads.

"Let me give you a tour," he said.

I followed him to his work table, which was pushed up against a window on the north-facing wall and framed a view of the nineteenth-century wooden barn that sat on my parents' property—a structure my father had repeatedly sketched. His tools were spread across the desk surface: paintbrushes, pencils, and felt-tipped markers were corralled into silver soup tins, pots of paint lined the windowsill, several inkwells and a clutch of fountain pens sat at the far side of the table, and beyond that, a glass jar filled with water that had been muddied by paint. Finished drawings lay in modest piles on the right side of his work table and were fanned out across the cushions of a small sofa in the middle of the room, as well as on the seat of a high-backed chair. There was nowhere for a visitor to sit down.

"I've been working on a series of cactus sketches," he said, picking up a drawing from the pile on his desk. "Your mother says I should call this series *Organic Forms*. No more open graves."

He tilted his head toward me and winked.

"I was never in style," he said, then reconsidered. "Maybe I was cool once? I guess there was that time I was on the cover of *artscanada* in, ah, the seventies?"

The cactus drawings, inspired by a trip to Mexico the previous winter, were for a one-man show happening in July. The gallery owner had been by earlier in the week. He'd chosen paintings right off the wall of my parents' home.

"He took the rose-coloured tondo," my dad said, meaning the circular-shaped oil painting from a series he'd started in the mid-sixties but rediscovered in the late 2000s and finished in 2010.

"I hope it doesn't sell," I said, half-serious. I had a sense of attachment to certain of my dad's works. The tondo, which is a Renaissance term for a circular piece of art, had hung on the wall outside the drawing room for several years. I'd come to associate this work with my dad's later life, that surprising time when he began to use the colour pink—but, also, a time when he began to paint less. The works he did complete had taken on a special, near-sacred quality.

"Have you been painting this winter?"

"Not a lot. The studio is cold," he said. "And, it's small. I can't make big works."

"The size of the studio? That's why you're making smaller paintings?"

I was unconvinced.

He considered this.

"Well, put it this way," he said. "I couldn't paint either the red *King and Queen* or the black *King and Queen* now because I couldn't lift them. Back then I was doing seven or eight large paintings at a time. They were about eight or nine feet, and they had frames on them, but I could move them. I could pick up a painting a little below the centre, grab it, and shuffle it."

I imagined my dad in his forties, wearing his paint-smeared blue overcoat, bending, lifting, and twirling his giant paintings in one fluid, balletic movement.

"They were the biggest," he said. "And the best."

"*King and Queen?*"

"Yes," he said. "Especially the red one."

I was surprised to hear my dad say that he considered this to be his best work. Not because I disagreed, but because I didn't know you could choose the best among your own works of art. It seemed a little like favouring one child over another. Also, something about it felt defeatist. What was left to strive for if the pinnacle of your career was behind you? The thought panicked me.

"What about your work now, though?" I asked him, pressing. "Couldn't your best be yet to come?"

"It would be nice to think that the best painting I'm ever going to do is still waiting to be done, but I have a hunch that it won't..." He trailed off, glancing at the pile of drawings on his desk then back at me. "The best work on paper might be, because I'm working on paper, but you can't will a masterpiece."

WHAT HAS BEEN REPEATEDLY documented is a sudden bolt of brilliance late in an artist's life. In music, this is called the "swan-song" effect. The author of a 1989 study published in the journal *Psychology and Aging* looked at more than 1,900 works by nearly 200 classical composers and identified what he termed the "swan-song phenomenon" — a burst of creative output in the final stage of life that is often considered the musician's best work. Richard Strauss composed *Four Last Songs* as his finale. Together, the four songs that comprise the posthumous album are my father's favourite musical work. I once asked him to describe it to me.

"I can't," he said, his eyes welling with tears. "It's too beautiful."

The crowning example of a swan song in visual art may be Monet's *Water Lilies*. "He was an old man in a hurry," says Ross King. "I guess that's one of the things you do when you get older—you begin thinking about posterity and also wanting to make an artistic statement. You don't have decades left and, therefore, you have to synthesize what you've learned and create a final masterpiece or series of masterpieces."

Consider Nunavut-based artist Elisapee Ishulutaq, whose drawings and prints depict life in the Arctic. Her early works were typically smaller than two by three feet. Then she learned to use oil sticks, and her canvases expanded. She began working in a drastically different scale when she reached her mid-eighties. In a 2010 review, *Georgia Straight* visual-art critic Robin Laurence wrote, "The oil stick medium seems to have given the octogenarian Ishulutaq license to bust out of all constraints of colour, form, and scale." In 2016, at-ninety-one years old, Ishulutaq created her largest work to date. *In His Memory* is a four-panel oil stick drawing that stretches thirty feet. It's a monumental work to honour a harrowing event: the images depict the aftermath of a young boy's suicide in the 1990s and its impact on Ishulutaq's small Arctic community. In the third panel, small, brightly jacketed people retreat from a modest cairn topped with a cross. Two members of the group, a young child and an adult, reach for each other. It's a small gesture of hope, writ large.

I VISITED HUGH MACKENZIE about a week after the conversation with my mother. I wanted to ask him about Dot—about her career, and her art—but when I did, he hung his head.

"Everyone had their roles then," he said, referring, I think, to the early and middle years of their marriage— often, the very period of time when artists are fuelling their careers. "She was so talented, and I don't think I really appreciated that. So, I'm ashamed. I'm ashamed by that." He said he was ashamed so many times that I also felt remorse, sorry to have mucked around in the unchangeable past. He was ninety-two years old. He lived in a care home. The walls were taupe; the trim and the coffered ceilings were painted cream. There was the clatter of crockery on the morning I visited, teacups and saucers being stacked, causing shrill, near-painful decibels of sound to drift up from some unseen canteen below as I signed my name on a guest log at the front desk. Much of Hugh's artwork concerned the grit of the city—the whorl of the circular parking garage captured in a dark etching, the steel crosses of an extension bridge reproduced in a black-and-white print. He felt the urban landscape had "a raw power to it." His new space, in the heart of an expensive shopping district, was designed to be impenetrable by the city that surrounded it; the concrete, crowds, and traffic were barely visible through the front-door windows, edged in brass, the panes clouded. Upstairs, his room was a distilled version of the home on Macpherson Avenue that he'd shared with Dot. There was the ornate, gold-framed mirror from Mexico with the crack running down the centre that had hung in the foyer, and a pared-down version of his art collection: his own works; a small, round floral print that my father made with my brother, Marsh; several paintings made by Hugh's students; and many of Dot's watercolours.

"I miss her so much," he said. "It's painful." I thought of how my mother had said, emphatically, that Dot and Hugh loved each other. That their marriage had lasted when nearly all the other couplings of their generation had fallen apart, my father and his first wife included. I'd brought a photograph of Dot's *Bowl with Lemons* with me. Hugh hadn't seen it in years, and greeted the work like an old friend.

"Oh, look at that," he said, his eyes lighting up. "I'm biased, I know, but it's worth any Mary Pratt."

Some of Dot's work had been exhibited, posthumously, alongside Hugh's work in a show celebrating his eighty-eighth year. Nothing changed after that, however. Dot's paintings remained in private collections — and Dot herself, unknown.

THE SUBTERRANEAN STUDIO on William Street and the life that we lived above it was dismantled the year I turned seven, when we moved to Wellesley, a small town in the country named for a long-dead British general. We were a twenty-minute drive from our first home, but our family landscape had altered radically. My older sisters stayed in the city. Allyson had married and was expecting her third child that year. Robin had moved in with her boyfriend. Also, my brothers, older teenagers by then, began visiting less. We rarely met their train on Friday nights, waved them off on Sundays.

Dot painted my portrait the summer we moved. We sat together in the living room of the new home. Late-afternoon light from the side window fell across the bridge of my nose, illuminating my profile. My dirty-blonde hair was cropped to just above my shoulders that summer, short for the first time. My arms were thin and brown. I was wearing a white button-up blouse with short, puffed sleeves and a scalloped collar. My head was propped against a threadbare diamond-pattern quilt that was thrown over the arm of our living room sofa. The dark mahogany back plate, carved by my under-taker ancestors, ran alongside my prone body. There was another throw underneath me, a pink floral piece of batik that protected the couch from our deranged, greasy dog. I was looking down, my eyes on the pages of the book I held in my hands. The cover isn't visible, but based on my age I might guess that it was one of the *Emily* books by L. M. Montgomery, or maybe something featuring Francine Pascal's *Sweet Valley High* twins, of whom I was deeply enamoured, all the more so as my mother disapproved of the series.

Not all of this is in the portrait. The painting is mostly of my face, with a hint of the diamond quilt behind my head. I knew the bulk of the details from memory and from the snapshot that I'd discovered. Both in the portrait and in the photograph, it seems as if I'm unaware that I'm being painted, or, at least, I am unbothered by sitting still in what must have been an exercise in patience for a young child. It wasn't that being painted was a regular occurrence: it was not. But it was not unusual, in my childhood, to sit parallel to an artist engrossed in the act of creation, quietly lost in their imagination and craft. No doubt my mind was elsewhere as this work of art was made, focused on my book, or maybe drifting off the page to think of the new school I'd be attending in the fall, or pondering the sudden disappearance of my many siblings.

After purchasing the new home, my father had hired local Mennonite tradespeople to build him a studio in the backyard. It looked like a mid-sized barn with large glass windows. The interior was flooded with natural light. There was a back room for the table saw (I still had yet to touch the saw, and I never would) and there was a drafting table under a bank of windows that overlooked Wellesley Pond. In the central room there was a space with a grey-and-white-flecked linoleum floor where my dad worked on his sculptures and larger paintings, and beside this, on a high counter, were two sheets of Plexiglas that he used as giant palettes for his oil paints.

There was running water and a bucket-sized sink for rinsing rags and paintbrushes, although my dad continued to use turpentine to wash his hands. Also, there was now a fan for ventilation.

It was the biggest studio he'd ever had, ever would have, and the only one that had a place just for me. To the right of the front door there was a small work table and chair, and a space of blank wall for hanging finished art. Beside the table were tall drawers for keeping crayons, pencils, paints, and paper. I'd been granted permission, finally, to enter the studio. The position wasn't hard-won; I was the only child left at home. Still, I knew this marked a significant change in our relationship. I'd arrived, finally, at my father's side.

Although I would never be an artist, I would become a writer who occasionally wrote about artists. People assumed this was my mother's influence, and her love of reading and writing certainly shaped my interests as a young person, but it was my dad who encouraged me to tell stories.

For six years, I drove with my father from our home in the country to my elementary school in Waterloo. The drive from our town took about twenty minutes, sometimes longer in winter when the roads were precarious—icy and plagued by snowdrifts. Each morning, we drove through stretches of farmland, passing by tiny villages and hamlets christened by the European and Mennonite settlers, some with searing optimism, like the scattering of homes that was Lisbon or the crossroads called New Prussia. We'd travel through

Gad's Hill, Crosshill, and "Spin-out Corners," local place names mixing with our own coinages, small points in the natural world that contained family lore—like that icy bend in the road where my mother had lost control of our Le Car and wedged it into a snowbank. There was Goosetown, Queen's Bush, Shinglestettle, and Surasas Springs, none of which were much more than a dot on a survey map. There was the strip of houses named Bamberg, with its rumoured darkness: secret societies and candlelit marches. We drove by abandoned homes and fallow fields that sat next to industrious Mennonite farms with no electrical lines reaching to their barns or homes from the road. We'd pass buggies on the right, *slowly, slowly*, so as not to spook the horse. At the halfway point, I'd seek the peaked eaves of the shack where the ancient, quiet brothers lived with no power or running water, and, occasionally, I'd spot one of the brothers wandering the roadside, walking the ten kilometres to the closest town for food or to fetch the doctor. These men were rooted in an earlier time, as much a part of that landscape and its history as the maple trees, the timber-frame barns, and the ploughed fields.

I wove these places and people into stories that I told my dad on the mornings we drove together into the city. As we pulled out of town he'd offer a few basic plot points—a character, a place, a thing—but the rest was up to me. Using his suggestions, I'd tell a story timed to the length of our drive.

"Well done," he'd say, as we pulled into the parking lot at my school. "You did it again."

ON THE NIGHT AFTER I spoke with my dad in his drawing room in Colborne, I lay in the darkness willing sleep
in a bedroom that was crowded with my two children
and our dog. I was thinking about the conversation we'd
had that afternoon, how I'd asked my dad about the
present but he'd pulled me into the past. I remembered
how, at one point, he'd become confused about when
he'd painted *King and Queen*. He'd looked up and smiled,
as if surprised to see me.

"I made those big paintings when we lived on Central
Ave," he said. "God, you were young then."

"No," I countered. "You lived on Central Ave in
London, before I was born. You made the *King and
Queen* paintings on William Street, in Waterloo."

He was confusing me with one of my older sisters.
He was envisioning his house in London, Ontario, a
two-storey Italianate home of some historical interest
where he'd lived with his first wife and their four children during the 1960s and early 1970s.

"Of course," he said. "How could I forget?"

The life on Central Ave was a time I knew only in
black-and-white images by the late photographer Don
Vincent, taken of my siblings as children. There was
a gothic and sombre photograph of my two sisters sitting at a dining room table, the tall sideboard — the
one that sits under my father's haystack painting in my
parents' home now — visible in the background. They
are wearing cone-shaped straw hats. One is looking
at the camera while the other tips her head forward,
obscuring her face in a blur. In another, my brother

Marsh, a toddler in a white undershirt, sits on a too-big chair, toes stretched out toward the lens, eyes dark and round. My brother Aidan doesn't appear in these images. Being the youngest, he was probably asleep in his crib, or perhaps he was not yet born.

The other images, the public ones, were of Vincent's peers, including my father, taken at the height of a synergic arts movement in a city surrounded by farmland, far from Toronto, which had long been considered the epicentre of visual art. The London artists were making their own noise, drawing inspiration from their surroundings and from each other. In one photograph, young artists crouch in an empty room, looking at works on paper spread out across the painted floor. It is night, and the windows are dark. There are two babies in the background, one reaching for the other. Recently, I'd come across a photograph of my father from Vincent's collection that I'd never seen before. In it, he stares ominously through a gap in the open door of one of his sculptures. He's wearing his familiar overcoat, flecked with oil paint, but the wood panelling visible in the background is unfamiliar to me—as of course it would be, the photo dating from the 1960s, long before I was born. It might have been taken at the University of Western Ontario, where my father was the school's first artist-in-residence, and where he would later teach, but more likely it was taken in his home studio at the time—a place I couldn't even imagine.

I'd confirmed the dates that my father had lived on

Central Ave in London by checking an old art catalogue from a retrospective he'd had at the National Gallery of Canada in Ottawa. *King and Queen* is dated 1984, and by then, my parents were married, I was seven, and we lived in Waterloo. I wondered if this memory slip mattered. Also, why had I felt compelled to correct him? The shifting dates and time periods, the artwork made where and when, the conflation of children from his first marriage with the child from his second, their various stages and ages, there were a lot of threads to weave together.

Memory is a fiction. What can seem real and perfectly formed, detailed and true, can also be false. I learned this in my late twenties when I wrote a story for an anthology about fathers and daughters. In that essay I described the terrible fall I'd had while peering into my father's basement studio on William Street. Even now, I can envision my childhood self on the cellar stairs, crouched and hidden behind a painting. I can feel the thrill of being invisible twinned with the fear of being caught, as well as the urge to see more than the sliver of doorway allowed. I can feel myself inching closer, stretching higher, and I can feel the sudden give of the canvas that had shielded me from view.

I shared a near-final draft of the story with my father, and he telephoned me afterwards to talk about what I'd written. He told me that he liked the piece, and that he had only one comment.

"You never fell over one of my paintings in the basement."

"But I remember you standing over me," I said. "Marsh and Aidan were there, too."

"I don't think that happened."

"You don't remember me ruining one of your paintings?"

"I don't."

"Falling?"

"No, I'm afraid not."

It was possible that I had fallen at some point, but that it hadn't been as dramatic as I'd remembered. The painting undamaged, my injuries minor. Maybe this was why it hadn't remained etched in my father's mind, as it had in mine. Given my age at the time—somewhere between three and seven—it was also possible that it hadn't happened at all. I would never know. Unlike the dates of the *King and Queen* paintings, I couldn't check this against an old art catalogue. I asked my dad if I needed to rewrite the story, erase the misremembered scene. My father, understanding and wise, was generous in his response.

"It doesn't matter if I don't remember it that way, because it's your memory."

"Should I leave that scene in the story?"

"Yes," he said. "It's your story and you can write it however you like."

Corkboard

THE ROUND DINING TABLE moved with us to our
new home in Wellesley, where it was pushed
against one wall of the kitchen, leaving room for
only three chairs. In place of a fourth seat at the table
was a corkboard—five feet long and running from
the wainscotting to the ceiling—on which my father
pinned his works-in-progress. These were drawings
that would become finished pieces in themselves, or
idea sketches that might manifest into paintings or
sculptures. Some drawings remained on the board
for nearly a year, while others rotated out after a few
months. My father always worked in series, experi-
menting on a repetition of similar images, to keep the
work open-ended.

"You don't do just one painting of a horse," he said.
"You work on ten horses at once—and if you make
some kind of discovery on one of them you can try it

on the other nine. But if you just do one and finish it, you've taken the quality out of that idea."

Each drawing was different by some small or large mark, sometimes accidental. The ink blot in his drawing *Reclining Dog*, a rare figurative work—of a dog in ambiguous repose, possibly dead—was an accident, and yet it made the work more interesting. The undefined dot a question mark on the page. Plus, it was unavoidable. As my father wrote, in the introduction to a 2001 catalogue of a show that had included the dog sketch, "Really, what else could I do?"

The drawings on the corkboard were held in place by silver seamstress pins, the small heads of which would press into the flesh of your finger or thumb as you pushed them into the cork. Other life detritus occasionally found a home on these walls—dry cleaning tags, errant keys, a small silver roach clip with leather tassels that my mother found after I'd hosted a party when I was in high school.

"We'll just see who claims this," she'd announced, pinning the piece of paraphernalia to the board, where it remained until my parents moved from that house. Mostly, however, the board was the realm of my father's drawings, there for him to consider while he ate his meals. My mother and I faced each other at the dining table, but my father faced his work.

I NOTICED, ON A RECENT visit to my father's home in Colborne, that the corkboard was one-quarter the size of the one I remembered from childhood. The present board hung at eye level, a few paces opposite and slightly to the right of my father's place at the table, so that he was forced to angle himself just slightly away from his meal to look in the direction of his work. These were necessary compromises, the only way to incorporate the board into the open-plan layout of my parents' kitchen. In the past, there might have been more than forty works on the board, but now there was space for about fifteen. He kept a second corkboard of drawings at the family cottage, on an east-facing wall that ran opposite the dining table in a windowed porch. The cottage, which had been purchased by my maternal grandparents in the 1930s, sat on the shore of Lake Ontario, about a five-minute drive from my parents' home. There, the drawings blanched as they overwintered, the colours fading, some uniformly, others in irregular patterns. My father would return in summer to find his drawings changed by the elements— bleached by the bald winter sun, curled at the edges from the dampness of the lake—and take up where he'd left off the previous season.

The corkboards had a mercurial function that went beyond the act of looking at the drawings pinned there. They acted as a prompt for the unconscious mind. Repeatedly seeing the works while not intentionally working on them helped to prolong the creative process, to drag it unwittingly, even unknowingly, into the resting mind. It was an effort to capitalize on the fertile state of distraction—how a brilliant idea might arrive when you were arm-deep in dishwater, while showering, or even asleep. Paul McCartney said the melody to "Yesterday" came to him in a dream. This kind of creativity can't be willed. It is unprompted, and seemingly magic.

"That's when the good fairy is ambling around," my dad told me. We were sitting in his drawing room. It was early spring, 2017. "You remember her?"

As a child I had imagined her flitting about the corkboard at night, armed with tiny pens and paintbrushes.

"Yes, but tell me again."

"So, the good fairy is the part of your mind that is working even when you're doing something else, like driving your car, or eating," he said. "It's like there's somebody chewing. The trick is to get yourself thinking about something else."

This theory is based on the works of modern art and music theorist Anton Ehrenzweig, who wrote *The Hidden Order of Art*. My father employed the method with his students, telling them to turn their work to the wall overnight so that the good fairy would come in the dark hours and do her job.

"The next day, they'd see that it wasn't as bad as they thought," my dad said. "Nearly always, something had changed for them."

For all of his life, the corkboard had provided this service for my father, but now, a secondary function was revealing itself. Ideas had become elusive.

"They come," he said. "But just as quickly, they go."

Previously, he could hold on to an idea through his meal, while loading the dishwasher, or running an errand to the hardware store, completing daily tasks between the time of inspiration and execution. Now, this was proving more difficult. The board had become a kind of *aide-mémoire*.

"The notes are in the drawings, and that doesn't change," he said. "You may add to them but, nevertheless, it's there, literally in black and white."

THE SEMINAL STUDY ON creativity in old age was carried out in the mid-twentieth century by a psychologist named Harvey C. Lehman. In his 1953 book *Age and Achievement*, Lehman tracked artistic achievement in various disciplines over five-year periods, measuring success by the number of citations the creative person received in reference books, such as encyclopedias or textbooks. Lehman concluded that each art form has its own unique decline corresponding with age. Poets peaked in their mid-twenties, classical composers and painters withered in their thirties, and prose writers prevailed, if they were lucky, into their early forties. Old artists may possess wisdom, Lehman conceded, but their best work was behind them.

New research contests Lehman's methods and theories. For one, he drew conclusions based on texts that hadn't considered a large swath of the population, as women and people of colour were largely absent from these books. Also, in the late 1960s, psychological researchers discovered that older people are actually brimming with "crystallized intelligence" — cumulative wells of skills, knowledge, techniques, and style attained over their lifetimes.

In the eighteenth century, Japanese artist Katsushika Hokusai, known for his *Great Wave* woodblock print, claimed in the preface to his exquisite book of landscape woodcuts and drawings, *100 Views of Mount Fuji*, that only his late work mattered. "All I have produced before the age of seventy is not worth taking into account. At seventy-three I learned a little about the real structure of nature, of animals, plants, trees, birds, fishes and insects. In consequence when I am eighty, I shall have made still more progress. At ninety I shall penetrate the mystery of things; at a hundred I shall certainly have reached a marvellous stage; and when I am a hundred and ten, everything I do, be it a dot or a line, will be alive. I beg those who live as long as I to see if I do not keep my word."

In Hokusai's *Views*, Mount Fuji is sometimes a small protuberance in the distance, the action taking place in the foreground. In one, a woman with an infant tied on her back balances a round tray of packages on her head as she crosses a narrow bridge that divides a stream; the mountain rises to meet the sky far behind her. In another, the mountain is seen through spindly stalks of bamboo, and in a third, it is nearly obscured by the delicate and stylized froth on a cresting wave. Hokusai returned doggedly to his subject, seeing it anew with each painting and yet building on all of the views he'd painted before, each work informed by the last.

Hokusai was seventy-five when he wrote the passage about aging and the progress of his work. He'd

experienced a breakthrough, but not the flash of insight
we associate with genius, traditionally connected with
youth. He'd lived, studied, worked, and considered long
enough to truly see his subject matter, alive in his lines
and dots, and to understand it in new ways.

Some research suggests creativity is well-suited to
seniors. One study found that the thinning of the frontal
cortex that happens naturally in the aging process is
associated with fewer inhibitions, enabling creative
behaviour and thought—something I'd seen recently
when visiting my neighbour, Flo Little, a decorative
painter in her late eighties. Flo lives in the first-floor
apartment of the home across the street from ours.
Her son, Scott, and daughter-in-law, Margaret, occupy
the second and third floors. Scott and Margaret run an
antiques and historic architectural-detail shop called
Artefacts, in the nearby small town of St. Jacobs. It is a
warehouse of time and memory—objects from the past
century and beyond, salvaged from houses slated for
demolition. These things are both familiar and strange,
the warehouse a place for material ghosts to rest, await-
ing new life. Some of the pieces need restoration, or
"upcycling," by being sanded and painted, and Scott has
often hired his mother to help fill orders. No surface in
Flo's apartment is left undecorated: carefully chosen
colour decals line her kitchen shelves; she's embellished
the rise of the stairs that lead from her basement studio
to her first-floor living space; and the crown mould-
ing in the entranceway is a rich red, the baseboards
turquoise.

"I quit working for Scott," Flo told me, when I was having tea and Portuguese egg tarts at her apartment one morning. "People want the distressed look these days, and I can't do that. I can't paint something beautiful and then sand it away so you can barely see it. I'm just not going to do it anymore. I'm going to paint what I like."

I've only come to know Flo in her later years, and I suspect she was always certain in her thoughts, no matter if they strayed from the fashion of the day. But I wondered: could her age, that thinning of the frontal cortex that facilitated independent thought and creativity, be playing a role in her decision to create in the way she liked? We own a lovely stool painted by Flo: red legs alternate with turquoise spindles, and there is a delicate floral pattern on the seat. I'd hate to see any of this decorative work sanded away.

Another study suggested that Monet's cataracts, which he suffered from in old age, inspired new ways of seeing. An interesting proposition, but an artist's vision extends beyond what he or she sees with their eyes, and so the argument, while grounded in science, is artistically simplistic. It was the fruits of Monet's longevity—part crystallized intelligence, part imagination—that brought forth the *Water Lilies* series at the end of his life.

MEASURING CREATIVITY IS NOTORIOUSLY difficult, and no single approach is without shortcomings. In a literature review of 152 creativity studies, researchers from the University of Leuven in Belgium concluded that it was "an unsettled issue." The trouble with Harvey Lehman's study is that he favoured the output over the act. But *create* is a verb, an action. For older artists, who may work at a slower pace than before, this emphasis on output immediately puts them at a disadvantage. The study also overlooked the individualistic nature of making art. My father's imagination, murky and wild, is impossible to capture as it moves, as the mechanics of the idea form, bulldozing through the wall between the subconscious and conscious, distilling in the realm of the mind, then into a tangible finale, a work of art. This unfurling of idea to output— the inspiration and the process that take place while my father considers the drawings on the corkboard and sips his morning tea or takes a bite of toast with honey; or, when he walks away from the board, into that unconscious state championed in *The Hidden Order of Art*—cannot be quantified. Numbers cannot tell us about Renoir's desire to sketch a vase while dying, or how Turner engaged with light until taking his final breath. A slowed output, fewer hits or listings in a reference book—these are external measures of creativity, when the only true understanding of this elusive act is internal, invisible, and impossible to harness.

THERE CAN ALSO BE a creative stretching that happens late in life—something I witnessed in a performance by

Shakespearean actor Martha Henry in the spring of 2018 at the Stratford Festival. She was eighty when she played Prospero in *The Tempest*, a role nearly always reserved for actors in their later stages of life and career but, also, traditionally played by a man. More than half a century before, she'd played Miranda, Prospero's daughter, during her first summer at the festival. Back then, this gender switch would have been unthinkable. Initially, Henry balked when artistic director Antoni Cimolino approached her with the idea, but he was persuasive and she trusted him. Gradually she relented, coming around to the idea of reinterpreting Shakespeare, whose work she'd been engaging with all of her life. Reading the text from this new perspective, she discovered a line where Prospero speaks of crying while tending to his infant daughter and it struck her as particularly female. It wasn't that she believed the role was written for a woman; it was that she saw, for the first time, a more nuanced approach to gender in Shakespeare's work.

"All these years I've been selling Shakespeare short and I've been thinking that he simply wrote men and wrote women, and of course he writes wonderful men and he writes brilliant women, but I hadn't realized how much of the total human being there was in each part," Henry said.

On opening day she stood, powerful, on the edge of a cliff as the house lights dimmed and the stage lights slowly rose. She was the matriarch of the theatre and of the performance, magical, powerful, and fierce. Her cloak was made of swatches of fabric from costumes she'd worn as previous characters she'd played in her decades-long career with the theatre company. She made her way slowly, but with certainty, down the stairs and onto the stage. No one could take their eyes off her.

A month after this performance, I met with Martha Henry during a terrible summer rainstorm. We sat together in her office in the turn-of-the-century red-brick building that houses offices for the Stratford Festival, including the Michael Langham Workshop for Classical Direction, of which she is the head. On that morning, as we spoke of time, we were surrounded by history and memory—in the collected works of Shakespeare on her book-lined shelves, and the framed image of the bard directly opposite the door; and in the building that had a former life as a school and, in the more recent past, as the home of an art gallery where my brother Aidan once had a one-man show. When she spoke of the dead, she also spoke *to* the dead, as if they were there with us in her office. I, too, felt that they were there—her former colleague, actor William Hutt, who'd played Prospero to her Miranda that first year, and her muse, William Shakespeare—because she conjured them through intimate and casual conversation, and this, really, is what Henry has done all of her life. She has invoked characters from within herself, suspending the disbelief of her audience to the point where she disappears and the person they see before them is not Martha Henry, but Lady Macbeth, or Martha in *Who's Afraid of Virginia Woolf?*, or Prospero in *The Tempest*.

I'd asked about her memory—had it changed? Memory had been on my mind since my father had described his frustration with elusive ideas. *They come, but just as quickly they go.* Henry told me that she had noticed her memory morph, gradually, incrementally, through the years. An actor would be acutely aware of this muscle's fatigue, more so than most. She told me about her first season with the festival, when she was a young woman with long, dark hair and an oval face who'd landed a big role with a distinguished and successful theatre company for the summer.

"I learned the part of Miranda when I was twenty-two in the car driving to Toronto," she said, then waited a beat. "And I was driving."

"And now?"

"I go through the play every single day."

"What if you forget a line?"

"I just talk until Shakespeare comes back. Sometimes he's asleep, but he'll come back and touch me on the shoulder and say, 'Okay, come on.'"

A NEW APPROACH TO OLD AGE and creativity comes by way of a University of Chicago economics professor with an encyclopedic knowledge of art history named David Galenson, author of *Old Masters and Young Geniuses: The Two Life Cycles of Artistic Creativity.* Instead of looking at age, Galenson argues, we should be thinking in terms of approach. "There are two very different kinds of creativity," he told me when we spoke over the phone — and two types of creators. The first is a "conceptual innovator," a person who works from a single idea. These people tend to be radical: they may draft a quick sketch of a concept, and then, almost immediately after, assemble a masterpiece (consider Pablo Picasso and his *Les Demoiselles d'Avignon* or Andy Warhol's screenprints). Then there are "experimental innovators," who progress incrementally, learning with each sketch and layer of paint. These people often work on a series of drawings or paintings and angle toward an ideal vision that can feel just out of reach — think Rembrandt's late self-portraits, Cézanne's tenacious repainting of Mont Sainte-Victoire near the end, never quite believing he'd captured the natural mystery of the mountain, and Hokusai, patiently working towards an age where nature would become clear. Galenson's theory applies to the artist's process, but he also noticed a second trend: "There's a tendency for conceptual innovation to come early and a tendency for experimental innovation to come late."

Galenson speaks at a dizzying pace, his grand concepts made accessible with nuanced anecdotes. He references famous nineteenth- and twentieth-century artists with a fond exasperation usually reserved for an eccentric relative, as if he'd learned these life-snippets over coffee rather than through decades of extensive study and comparative work, graphing and charting artists' major successes and their corresponding ages by mining auction data and art history textbooks.

I'd described my father's practice to him, and Galenson's hunch was that he was an experimentalist because he works on a series of drawings of similar images, produces countless sketches, and does not have a set outline of where he hopes to end up; and because, too, he works every day, straight through most life events—faculty meetings, vacations, my wedding—barely stopping for life's basic intrusions, like eating.

"They never know what the question is so they try to learn everything they can," Galenson said. "The experimental painter doesn't know what time it is, just stays in the studio working because they are trying to make some discovery, whereas the conceptualist says, 'Oh, it's five p.m., suppertime, time to go home.'"

I told Galenson that the description of an experimentalist fit my father's approach in every way but one: he would never miss dinner. He has always had a keen enthusiasm for food. People love to cook for him. His nose twitches and his eyes light up when the main course arrives—whether he is at a dinner party or a roadside diner. "Talk to you later," he'll say, when tucking into a meal.

It wasn't an exact list of traits, Galenson explained; more tendencies that he'd noted that fit the profiles of two different sets of artists.

As he explained this to me, I imagined the kitchen in my childhood home where we took all our family meals, and an image of the corkboard materialized. It was true that my father never missed a meal; but he also worked through every single one.

THERE IS A THEORY concerning a shift in technique, medium, or scale that can occur in an elderly artist's work. It's called *Altersstil*, or "old-age style," initially recorded in seventeenth-century France and popularized by German art historians in the early half of the twentieth century. Some cultural critics, Kenneth Clark and Edward Said among them, claim that the same old-age-style characteristics appear across different forms and genres: an aging artist's work is seen by experts as increasingly abstract, spiritual, or ethereal, and the blurring of formal and informal styles is described as a nod to eternity.

But others in the art world say the idea that formal attributes can correspond with a creator's age is absurd. Galenson, for one, finds the idea ridiculous and ageist. "I mean, is there a 'middle-aged style'?" he asked, when I broached the topic with him. Galenson's school of thought argues that there are no definitive attributes that characterize late-stage creativity: yes, Hokusai, Rembrandt, and Goya were all geniuses in their later years, but each in their own incomparable way.

FOR MOST OF THE summer, there had been thirteen drawings on the corkboard at my father's house in Colborne. Today, my dad was unpinning three of them, images of crisscrossed black, thick lines that were inspired by a split rail fence along the road that led to the cottage. They'd been there for six months, and that morning, he'd seen something new in them. He was moving the sketches to his drawing room to begin a new project.

"Remember how we talked about the good fairy?"

"I do, why?"

"Well, it happened to me today. I did ten drawings and one or two are up there. I looked at one of them this morning," he said. "Then, I made a little drawing of it, a sketch, then another, and I can see a possible painting. While I was sitting here eating my breakfast I kept seeing it and I thought, this would be just a sky, very plain, and it may even have a frame around it, more than it has there," he said, gesturing to images that I could not presently see, but that would manifest later in a finished work of art.

"I had the idea," he said. "I think it will work."

"WHAT WOULD ONE DO when ideas failed or words refused to come?" asked Sigmund Freud, in a letter to Oskar Pfister, a Protestant minister with whom he corresponded over thirty years. "It is impossible not to shudder at the thought. Hence, in spite of all the acceptance of fate which is appropriate to an honest man, I have one quite secret prayer: that I may be spared any wasting away and crippling of my ability to work because of physical deterioration."

The same day that I had watched my father unpin several drawings from his corkboard, I asked him, tentatively, nervously, what he'd do if he was no longer able to draw. He didn't answer immediately; he weighed his words.

"I've considered that," he said, finally. "But then I stop thinking about it, because it would be terrible."

"So, if you weren't able to draw, it's not worth living anymore?" I asked, feeling bold.

"No."

That was as far as he was willing to discuss the matter.

House Among Trees

I T WAS LATE JUNE, 2017. I was with my father in the studio which sat behind a house my parents owned in Stratford, Ontario, a place they had purchased a few years before and had planned to move into some time in the next year. They'd been renting out the space until they felt it was the right time to move. Recently, the tenants had departed, so it seemed as if the perfect scenario had presented itself. My mother planned to be away in Ireland during the fall and winter that year, teaching at University College Dublin. My father, it was decided, would move into the Stratford home while she was gone, so that he could be near his children and grandchildren, all of whom lived within a forty-minute driving radius. Eventually, my parents would move there permanently, together.

My dad was wearing a light rain jacket that day; it had sprinkled earlier that afternoon. We'd gathered in his studio so that he could show me his new space for making art. I'd started recording him, on a whim, something I had been doing more and more as my father grew older.

He was telling me about two of his drawings that had been purchased by the Museum of Modern Art in New York in the late 1960s, and how one of them had been included in a group show more recently, called *Transforming Chronologies: An Atlas of Drawings*. The show and accompanying catalogue were grouped thematically, arranged by subject rather than chronologically or into successive art movements. My father's drawing, titled *Ambiguous Summer Forms*, was a series of small studies which could have been flora or fauna, but were recognizable as neither. There was a feeling of movement in the drawing, how trackside vegetation appears from the window of a moving train. His work was shown with other "tectonics," meaning landscapes, and in this curatorial configuration stood alongside Yves Tanguy, Gerhard Richter, André Derain, and, one of his artistic heroes, Paul Cézanne.

My father's new studio was shaded by a line of cedar trees and surrounded by an overgrown garden, once tended and carefully planned by some long-gone gardener. The tidy plots had spread and the flowers, growing wild, had intermingled with weeds, all of which were presently abuzz with pollinators. Inside the garden studio, there was a drafting table left behind by the previous owner, an architect. The long, narrow table ran along the front wall, then bent, like an elbow, and carried on along the east-facing wall. My father had spread out some drawing tools across the flat surface of the table—Prismacolor pencil crayons in a red velvet case with a gold interior, the crayons inside sharpened down to stubs. A miniature wooden suitcase with a metal clasp sat open to reveal a pot of black ink and three fountain pens. Beside this was a black, hardcover travel portfolio, fastened with duct tape, his initials— T. U.—stamped in white on the front. It held a modest stack of thick, blank paper, along with a few drawings he'd started earlier in the day: a many-paned window shrouded in weeds; one of his sketches of the beat-up war chest that belonged to my husband's ancestor; and what looked like a study for a new box. In the closet were three of my father's sculptures, bubble-wrapped and mysterious, bases stored on the left, the cabinet-like tops on the right. It was a space in flux, as my father began the shift between his current studio and this one.

My daughter was at the table, painting with a set of watercolours that were cracked and nearly gone, and my son was napping in an upstairs bedroom of the house. Andrew was inside with my mother.

"They showed the drawing in 1920."

He paused.

"No—damn."

He began again.

"As far as I know, the drawing wasn't shown until '26—'25, '26, something like that."

"Twenty-six what?"

"Ah, no, sorry."

He looked up, as if the answer might be in the air above his head. My dog, who'd been nosing about the garden, barked sharply in the background, breaking the silence.

"Sorry, twenty-*oh*-six, I think."

I remained silent, not understanding what he was trying to communicate.

"God," he said, rubbing his forehead. "Am I getting it wrong again?"

He was, he'd noticed, getting things wrong. The name of a street, the time of day, and, increasingly, the year had become difficult to decipher.

"The year?" I asked.

"Yes, 1926, I think. Well, anyhow, the drawings were included in the show in New York, not that long ago."

I should have heard it in the cadence of his stumble, but I could not. The years before the new millennium were clear. It was the years that came after, the years that began with twenty, that were confusing for him. He'd resisted them, even when they'd arrived, nearly two decades before. He felt their visual symmetry was off. At the turn of the twenty-first century, my father began dating his paintings using Roman numerals. He'd paused between the 20 and the 06, and because of this I hadn't understood—the drawing exhibit had happened in 2006.

He changed tack, and began talking about the landscape show, how he'd shared a wall with Cézanne, whose work, *House Among Trees*, was a spare poetic landscape, real or imagined, of the wildness of nature against the symmetry of a man-made structure.

"It's good company," my dad said, unspooling the emotion of the memory, dispensing with the dates. We moved past this moment and into the next. The minutes of the day ticked onward. The sun set, slowly. The light lingered into the night, staying bright longer than it had just the week before, the day before. It was almost summer. The days were getting longer.

That evening, as I ate takeout sushi with my parents, my husband, and our children, all of us crowded around a card table, we discussed the possibilities of the new home. There was an abrupt drop from the living room to the kitchen, and my son had fallen twice since we'd arrived that morning. Could we raise the floor, we wondered? What would that entail? What expense? We talked about which bedrooms worked for my parents, and which ones were for guests, or visiting grandchildren. They needed an area rug and some floor lamps for the dining room, and wouldn't a pair of armchairs be nice by the hearth? A temporary corkboard pinned full of my father's recent drawings hung opposite the table where we ate. There was already art on the walls: my father's second painting of our battered war trunk, *Strong Box II*, based on the sketch I'd seen in the studio that afternoon, hung above the fireplace, and, in the adjacent room, above the table where we were eating, was a tall, door-sized painting of flowers in a cage. There was always art where my parents lived, even in a transitional house like this one in Stratford. These pieces were from a recent show of my father's work in Toronto, delivered to Stratford after it had closed, instead of to their present home in Colborne. Despite knowing this, I felt as if the art had manifested from nothing, grown there, appeared like magic.

The talk turned to other things — the end of the school year for my daughter, what we might do during her summer vacation, and how I'd been accepted into a writing residency program in Banff that July, and which dates I needed my parents to help with childcare while I was away. These were the issues of the present, and the furniture choices and renovations were decisions for the future. There would be more time for these discussions. This is what we believed.

Two months later, I arrived at the Stratford house on a Saturday morning with my two children, lay a blanket on the floor (there were now even fewer pieces of furniture), and opened my laptop before them so that they could watch cartoons, leaving me free to begin the task of dismantling the skeletal life that had been set up within the walls of the home and studio. I made an inventory of the artworks that were there — the paintings on the wall, the boxes wrapped in bubble wrap in the studio closet. They would need to be shipped back to my parents' current home. I emptied the cupboards and fridge and scrubbed all the surfaces clean, filled boxes with plates and cutlery to give to charity, and mopped the floors. In these acts, I erased the idea of that space. My parents would never live there. The garden studio would not be where my father spent his third act.

A FEW DAYS AFTER we spoke in the garden studio, my father returned home and visited a geriatrician. He took some tests—drew, or failed to draw, a clock—and answered some questions. He was given a possibility, although it was one he'd already acknowledged, decades before, after his father's death from Alzheimer's disease, when my father began taking supplements of ginseng and something called Memory Fx, and, more recently, with his brother, who'd experienced dementia-related memory loss until his death in 2013.

Near the end of my grandfather's life, he regained his memory, only once that I know of, while dancing with my mother in our living room in Wellesley. He said, "I've lost everything." Fifteen years ago, I'd seen my father's brother, on the subway in Toronto, and he'd looked at me, bewildered, when I told him my name. He'd sent an email later that day. *Of course I knew it was you.*

My father's struggles with memory, his ideas that lifted and left, the words that escaped him, and the difficulty understanding numbers—these were all early signs of dementia, and this had now been confirmed. There had been other clues—how my father had mixed me up with my older sister, believing that I'd lived in London with him, which would have been nearly two decades before I was born. How he'd found it difficult, recently, to hold on to his ideas between spark and execution. Also, there had been a years-long struggle regarding the possible acquisition of one of his paintings by the Art Gallery of Ontario, where he'd found himself at an impasse with a new curator.

"He's waiting for me to die," he'd said, handing me a stack of correspondence regarding the matter, hoping I'd intervene.

The painting, *Allegory*, which he'd made in 1962, was a mysterious tangle of earth and weed set in a fantastical, deep-blue landscape. It had travelled to art fairs and won prizes, but had been "under consideration," sitting in limbo in the gallery's basement, for nearly five years. The new curator had promised to visit my father's studio to discuss the matter, and to see his new works, but after a series of plausible life excuses—family, work, health—the curator had admitted the visit would never happen. It was a blow. After going over the correspondence, I'd met with the curator. I'd arrived expecting to face a villain, but instead sat across from a balding man in his late forties wearing shorts and Blundstone boots—he looked like any number of the fathers I saw every morning dropping their children off at my daughter's school. He told me that he was taking a new direction, addressing gaps in the gallery's collection. I couldn't argue with his approach, although I felt the succession of curators had let my father's file slip through the cracks. My dad had had a personal relationship with the previous curator, but that man had since retired. This is an occupational hazard for older artists: the curators, art dealers, and even critics who are their colleagues do not work forever, as artists do. And so, for my father, over the past two decades there had been a personnel shift in almost every aspect related to the promotion, selling, procuring, and showing of his art.

Many retired. Plenty died. The gatekeepers change, but the artists remain the same.

"It's not personal," the curator said. But of course, for my father, when it came to his art, it was always personal.

The gallery and curator had mismanaged the situation, but in the past, my father might have asserted himself and finalized the process, one way or another. *Difficulties with problem-solving.* This could explain, in some part, why the issue with the painting dragged on for so many years, and why he'd felt powerless to address the problem. I'd read that long-term memories remain sharp, particularly foundational memories, and thought of how I'd struggled, during our conversations, to steer him into speaking of the present. Now I understood that it wasn't my fault, that my father would always end up back on the MS *Hanseatic*, heading to Europe for the first time, his grant money exchanged into traveller's cheques that were folded into his pocket. It was a period more profound than childhood, more important than graduating from art school or being signed by the country's foremost art dealer in his early twenties. It was on that ocean liner, and the voyage that followed, that his purpose solidified and his life as an artist truly began.

Before his visit with the geriatrician, my father's condition hadn't had a name. He'd referred to it as the trouble with his memory, or the problem of forgetting. The clinical name, dementia, is an umbrella term for a series of symptoms caused by diseases affecting the brain, symptoms manifested in difficulties with language and problem-solving, and, of course, memory loss. It's a common disease. It happens to one in ten people in their mid-sixties, one in three in their eighties. There are 50 million people living with dementia globally, a number that is projected to triple by 2050. It startles, though. When it happens, it catches us all unaware.

The geriatrician told him that it would be fine for my father to stay alone while my mother was in Europe, and, also, that he could still safely drive a car. Moving to a new home, however, was not a good idea. He'd explained that shifting the known world of a person in the early stages of dementia could wreak havoc. Making art, however, could in some ways be a panacea, a memory life-raft.

Keep drawing, the doctor told my father. Above all, keep drawing.

IN A 2017 STUDY published in the *Journal of Neuropsychology*, researchers used fractal analysis on the work of seven different artists to see if they could anticipate which of them might experience cognitive deterioration. They looked at age-related variations in over two thousand different works, analyzing their fractal dimensions—meaning the patterns unique to the creator. Some, but not all, of the artists whose works were examined had been diagnosed with neurodegenerative diseases later in life. The researchers discovered that they could predict which artists would develop diseases like Parkinson's or Alzheimer's based on infinitesimal changes in their brushstrokes. Previously, fractal analysis had been used in the art world to separate forged works from originals; now it seemed the future of an artist's health was also written into their art.

This study seemed of the moment, when so many of us were spitting into small plastic vials and mailing them off to large conglomerates who'd first steal our most precious information — what was written in our DNA — and then tell us both the story of our past and, should we tick that box, what was written into our future. What disasters awaited, lurking in the wings of our lives? This seemed like burdensome information; there was no real way to prepare for memory loss, nor any true indication of how the diseases that cause dementia might affect each individual.

The images featured in the study showed the kinds of changes in art that you don't need fractal analysis to identify — thicker, stronger brushstrokes, a more naive, simpler style, a realist's drift into abstraction. There was a magazine illustrator who visited Venice every year and each time painted the Bridge of Sighs. His images became more simplistic as the years passed and his disease progressed. The early watercolours were detailed and colour-filled. Cartoonish but realistic. The final work, done in pink on white, showed only a repeated pattern of spare architectural details, and yet it felt truer than the previous paintings, the essence of the bridge expressed in a way that the realistic images hadn't achieved. It was as if the artist had been set free.

Other examples were bleak. London-based artist William Utermohlen had painted his self-portrait repeatedly as he grew further into Alzheimer's disease. Over time, his face slowly distorted—his jowls were drawn downwards, his mouth gradually set in a frown, and his hollowed eyes grew dark and vacant. In some his skin was a jaundiced yellow, and in others he'd turned ash-grey. The works grew increasingly abstract until the final portrait, a black-and-white pencil sketch of his face with a cavernous fissure running from forehead to jaw-line. His features were shadowy and rearranged; some had been rubbed out. He had become unrecognizable.

I was alone in my kitchen, late at night, reading everything I could find on artists with dementia. I looked at Utermohlen's final portrait, backlit on my computer screen, for a long time. Then, I turned away and wept.

AS A CHILD, I spent spring nights awake in the dark, unable to sleep, fearing that my father was going to die. He was in his forties when I was born and I understood this to be incredibly old. I was confused about the realities of aging, but I did have a sound grasp of our family's difference. My father was nearly twenty years older than most of my friends' parents, and no one had adult siblings, as I did. I've occasionally met people with a similar family choreography since, but in the late seventies and early eighties, in our years in the city, and certainly in the small village we eventually moved to, our family was unusual. I can't say exactly when this knowledge took shape, but it was possibly around age four, when I started kindergarten. On one of my first days, I'd returned from school, bewildered and wanting answers. Nobody else's father had a studio, I told my parents. I said it in a way that suggested I felt these other fathers were at a loss, impoverished and left wanting. This was normal, my parents assured me. They explained that my father was different, in many ways, from the other fathers of the children in my kindergarten class. Over time, I realized that my dad might have a place to paint, but the other fathers had their youth. So, particularly when he was away in Europe in the spring, I worried he was nearing death.

Then, one night, something terrible did happen to my father, to both of my parents, when they were travelling in France. I was staying with my older sister, Robin, but I'd been out at an all-ages nightclub with a friend. I'd been drinking beer with two girlfriends in a nearby ditch before entering the club, along with two strange boys who'd trailed us there. The boys posed a far greater threat than the consuming of two bottles of beer shared between five people, and it's possible the police knew this as they watched us disappear over the hump of the ditch. They did confiscate the beer, but sent us inside with a warning: "If we catch you again, we're calling your parents."

I'd given them my real name and my sister's phone number, but I'd lied about my age. I said I was sixteen, which was still three years shy of the legal drinking age, but I felt the officers might insist on taking me home if I admitted to being only thirteen. Terrified of being found out, I nearly fainted the next morning when my sister told me that she had to speak with me about something important. However, it was not about the underage drinking fiasco. My parents had been held up at knife-point during an evening walk outside the small French town where they'd been staying. My father had resisted the thieves, refusing to release the straps of my mother's purse, which he'd been carrying because it was over-packed and heavy. He'd fallen to the ground while the men kicked him, repeatedly, in the side and in the head.

My mother had shrieked—not at the men, but at my father: "Give them the fucking purse, Tony!"

My parents were down one passport, and out of money, but otherwise fine, despite the assault. My sister felt she should tell me the story in case I'd overheard her on the telephone with our father. I was rattled, certainly, imagining my poor father being kicked on the ground, refusing to release the handbag like a dog with a bone, but I was also relieved. The worst that I could have imagined had finally happened, and he'd lived. Also, the police never called my sister to report my under-age drinking. It felt like a clean escape—for both of us.

I stopped worrying about my dad after that, even as the years ticked on and he moved closer to eighty. He was robust, a survivor, a "pleasure hog" as my mother described his general enthusiasm for art, food, golf, and life in general. He was steady, and impervious.

MY PARENTS FELT THE diagnosis should remain a secret, even from their closest friends. This was mostly a social decision—my father didn't want to be treated any differently by his peers—but it also related to my father's career. Although he was in his eighties, he was still working, which meant that he'd need to continue dealing with the business of art. He didn't want to be brushed off as "ga-ga," irrelevant to conversations about his legacy or the organization of shows of his present work, the most recent of which was happening the weekend after his diagnosis.

The change in my father's cognitive abilities wasn't without precedent among artists. The most prominent example of a working artist with dementia was American artist Willem de Kooning. De Kooning was diagnosed with dementia in 1985, and he made more paintings that year than in any other. While dementia affects the declarative memory—the ability to recall names, facts, the last time you ate—it has less impact on procedural memory, which is inherent to the physicality of making art. Brush to canvas, hand to plaster—these are travels along a well-worn pathway of the brain. As the disease progressed and the trappings of cognition fell away, de Kooning wasn't able to produce the day of the week, or even the month, nor could he remember proper nouns, the closest town, the name of a friend; and yet, he was calmly at ease in contemplating his work, and adept when facing the easel. As time wore on, his assistants might rotate his canvas for him, so that he could paint a forgotten corner. He had started to focus only on what was directly in front of his eyes. They also diversified his palette when he relied too heavily on the same three colours.

"We all started getting anxious that he was only interested in red, yellow, and blue," one of his assistants confided to de Kooning's biographers. "For some reason his palette was becoming more and more limited."

Their interference makes it impossible to know what de Kooning's work might have been, unassisted. I'm empathetic to their impulse to intervene, but I also wonder why his assistants couldn't have allowed de Kooning to paint like an artist who also had dementia. We are crushingly ableist in our worldview. A disabled person making art might be seen as peculiar or as remarkable, but rarely are they perceived as being on a level playing field with able-bodied artists.

There is more white space in de Kooning's late works than in his earlier paintings, and, as remarked on by his studio assistant, blue, red, and yellow pervade the canvas. There is a new airiness to his work, a playfulness. There is a sense of whimsy where there was once a foreboding. His brushstrokes are fluid and curved, less frenzied than in the past.

MoMA showed a group of his final works in 1997, a decade after the artist's death, and critics reacted venomously. Art writer Allan Stone said it was "outrageous that MoMA gave the seal of approval" for the show, adding that the paintings were clearly done by a person "operating on one cylinder." Even de Kooning's sympathetic admirers felt the late works were important only as a historical record, and not as fully realized works of art.

Today, as de Kooning's late works are being fêted and given dizzyingly high financial values, critics still cannot accept this period as artistically significant.

"I look at the works, and look again. I remain wholly unconvinced that they represent a great, late flower-ing," wrote London-based art critic Michael Glover, reviewing a show of de Kooning's paintings from the mid-'80s, mounted at a commercial gallery in 2017. He felt the gallerist, who effusively praised the late works, was a pawn in a game of high-stakes art sales. She'd spoken of their sparseness, their flow and colour, citing these paintings as evidence of an artist's late, and last, bloom.

It matters because of money, Glover argued—because of the fear of overvaluing work without grounding it in merit. Neither Glover nor any other prominent critic accepts de Kooning's late works as significant to his oeuvre. No wonder my parents chose secrecy.

It was in the work of dementia-care researcher Pia Kontos that I found comfort. Kontos speaks of the med-icalized lens through which the general population views those with dementia, and how it reduces them "to a catalogue of cognitive deficits and behaviour dis-orders ignoring other facets of what it is to be human." This approach, she writes, works to further facilitate the loss of self that people with dementia fear. What Kontos proposes is radical, flying in the face of what we believe about dementia. The underlying theme to

almost every theory on de Kooning's continued creativity—from the idea that making art helped the artist
recover from Alzheimer's, to the notion that he was
misdiagnosed, to the belief that he wasn't the architect
of his own creativity and that the works were done
by studio assistants—is a persistent belief that creativity and cognitive impairment can't co-exist. Based on
her research, Kontos feels differently. She asks, what if
de Kooning painted "despite his dementia"?

I searched for images of de Kooning as he was late
in life. I felt that seeing the artist at work in his studio
might proffer some vision for my father's future. If
that were the case, it looked okay. De Kooning had a
shaggy white mop of hair, and was often pictured in
paint-splattered overalls, sitting in his rocking chair or
facing his latest work-in-progress in the airy, church-
like interior of his East Hampton studio. The studio
was flooded with natural light and filled with his giant
canvases—propped on easels and hanging on the soaring white walls above his workspace. Everywhere he
turned, he would have seen himself in the manifestations of his creativity.

I understood my parents' desire for secrecy, but
also railed against a society that required this of them.
Each time I thought about the critic who'd referred to
de Kooning as an artist "operating on one cylinder," or
the more recent critics who refused to see the value in
his late works, I grew angrier. It felt personal now. I felt
protective of de Kooning—long dead, of course—and
of my father.

Thinking of this recent revelation, I remembered something my mother said following the *Allegory* debacle with the curator. She'd summed up my father's response to the rejection of his work—"He's disappointed"—but pulled the rest of his life sharply into focus. "The thing about your father is that you can do anything to him, call him a boy genius at twenty-four, accept or refuse his work, and he's always going to keep making art. Every day. If he didn't," she paused, then sighed. "Well, I guess he'd die."

This was, for the most part, true, with one, terrible exception, a period of time when my father's studio fell silent, his works-in-progress stilled, brushes sitting quietly in the silver coffee tins, oil paints slowly going dry. Nearly twenty years has passed since, but I think of this time still, a shadow on the periphery of my memory, nearly every day.

Untitled

It was a friday morning in late September, 2001. I was twenty-three years old. My father had stopped by my apartment in Toronto to help me hang some bamboo blinds I'd bought for the windows of a small sunroom that I used as an office, and where guests occasionally slept on a narrow white cot. I was a few weeks into my second year of journalism school. I had been working towards becoming a news reporter or a magazine writer, angling for the implied stability of learning a trade. I felt I could be a writer, but I could also earn a living. Having been raised in a family of artists, I understood the precarious nature of artistic work. I wanted to participate in art, but I also wanted to escape its uncertainty.

I'd taken the day off from school to visit with my father, and that afternoon we went to see some new shows at a scattering of commercial galleries in the city's east end, and then visited the Art Gallery of Ontario to see the recently opened exhibition of paintings by British artist Stanley Spencer. I don't remember seeing this show, though I do remember the restaurant on Baldwin Street where we ate lunch at a corner table, and the way the fall light spilled over the place settings. I remember saying goodbye to my dad outside the gallery, on the steps, vaguely aware that he would be driving to another art show that evening, in a city about two hours west of Toronto where he planned to stay the night. I also remember the coloured-pencil drawings of oversized vegetables on display at one of the small east end galleries we visited; and yet to this day I only know we saw the Spencer exhibition because the ticket stub sat on my office desk for nearly a year afterward. And so, years later, coming across Spencer's work at the Tate Britain in London, it was as if I were seeing his paintings for the first time: an end-times resurrection in a small-town cemetery, crowded with the undead rising from their graves; a nude self-portrait with the voluptuous naked wife of his doomed second marriage; his final self-portrait, made five months before his death at sixty-eight, looking cock-eyed and deadpan, an intense and visually precise work.

My father had brought his own tools to my apartment, as I had nothing so sensible as a screwdriver or hammer at my home. The sunroom was a small space, and we climbed over stacks of books, leaned over my desk, and crouched on the thin bed in an effort to fasten the blinds into place. It was more difficult to manage than either of us had expected. The blinds were larger than the window frames and abutted at the corners so that you needed to lower them and roll them back up in a certain order.

"Like this," my father demonstrated for me, rolling the three blinds down, one at time, from left to right, and then rolling them back up again and tying them neatly into place.

Eight months later, I was packing to move to a new apartment and, using the tools that my father had left behind, I began to unscrew the blinds, wrenching them from where they'd been attached to the window frames. As I pulled the first scroll free, I caught my breath. It felt as if I'd been slapped, hard, on the back. My heart began to beat rapidly, and I was enveloped by a sorrow so inky and thick I couldn't see through it. Rattled, and afraid I might faint, I crawled onto the cot. There was memory embedded in those inanimate objects, in the energy my father and I had expelled while hanging them, in the turn of the screw, the hammer's swing, the strength used to hold them up as the other person fixed them into place. There was the memory, also, of how dusk fell that night and I lowered the blinds for the first time, one after the other, as my father had instructed, affording privacy where once I'd been a beacon of light hovering above the street, at the foot of a park, for all to see as I worked at my computer late at night, writing. How I'd un-scrolled the final blind and rested it on the sill when I heard the telephone ring. How my boyfriend at the time had answered, but then gone strangely silent. How

I'd come out of the office to find him holding the phone away from his body, as if it were black magic, dangerous and wild, and how he'd slowly brought this newly strange object toward me, but said nothing, his mouth open so wide that I could see all of his teeth. How I'd listened as my mother's voice, crushed and hoarse, tinny and far away, told me that my oldest brother, Marsh, had died.

The blinds stayed lowered for the next two weeks, shrouding my various writing tools — my handheld recorder, the tiny tape paused; a clutch of pens; and a lined reporter's pad, open to notes I'd made during an interview with a young fashion designer for a story that I would never write.

A year and a half before my brother died, on Saturday, March 4, 2000, we were all in Toronto — my two sisters, Robin and Allyson, my brother Aidan, and my parents. My father had an afternoon opening at the Moore Gallery, which was in a former garment warehouse on Spadina Avenue, and that evening Aidan was in a group show at the Loop Gallery in the west end of the city. Aidan had created a world in the window of the show space, a maquette-sized town of debauchery and wild abandon. It reminded me of the paper towns he used to build in our fireplace in Wellesley when he'd come to visit on weekends. These small cities were elaborate and story-rich in their various shops and homes, in the relationships between their neighbours, and in how my brother would narrate their terrible collective fate. The inhabitants would howl with rage when their homes and shops burnt down; they hollered and moaned and used terrible, filthy language. In the end, there was nothing left but ashes. Aidan was a teenager and I was in elementary school, and this was as close as we'd ever come to playing together. It was intoxicating. Now, in the gallery window, was another one of his make-believe worlds, also made of paper, but not burning.

We stood outside despite the cold, marvelling at Aidan's small city for a long time. Robin called Marsh repeatedly on her cell phone, but he didn't pick up. He lived in Toronto, and he had said he'd come. We were all there, together, and we wanted him to join us. Even Allyson had come, and she was rarely at these events, having five children to look after by then. One of my father's colleagues stopped to speak with us and Robin impulsively introduced me to her as Allyson. The woman raised her eyebrows. She knew me. She knew I wasn't my sister. We were seventeen years apart and we looked nothing alike. No one was behaving well. It was as if the adult children had gone feral, reverted to a childhood that we'd never, at least not all of us together, shared. My friend Ciara was with me and, years later, she told me how upsetting it was to watch us call Marsh, each one of us leaving messages that berated my brother for his absence. But how could we have known?

Of course, we knew. Not that he would die, but that he was drinking. We knew because he called us late at night. We knew because sometimes we couldn't answer the phone, understanding what awaited us on the other end. During one call, deeply distressing, I had the eerie sensation that I was speaking to a stranger, that I'd been erased, and he'd forgotten who, if anyone, was holding the receiver on the other end. Now we phoned and phoned and phoned him, and he was the one who refused to answer. We wanted him to know this: Aidan's work was brilliant that night. It shone like the stars.

It was around this time that a counsellor at an addiction treatment centre met with my father and brother, looked into the yellowing whites of Marsh's eyes, and told him his liver was failing, and that he would die if he didn't stop drinking immediately. Facts can't force an addict into rehabilitation. Marsh was adamant as he and my father left the centre and walked back to their car.

"I'm not going there."

What was remarkable to me later, reflecting on the story about the meeting with the counsellor, was that my brother had agreed to go with my father to the centre in the first place. Was he truly considering checking himself in, or had he done it to please my father? I'll never know. The addiction centre wasn't far from where I lived about fifteen years later. I glimpsed it, once, while visiting a friend. We were walking with our children to a park near her house. It was winter; the ground was snow-covered and we could see our breath. The centre, foreboding and castle-like, stood across the river, nestled amongst leafless trees. I let my friend walk on with our children while I stared, frozen, unable to move, and took in the contours of the building that had once held a possibility, however spare, of hope. Who was saved there, I wondered? What life trajectories were changed there, and what did that look like, and how, and where, were those people now? I didn't think of these nameless recovered addicts with resentment, only with wonder. Because our story had ended so differently, I found theirs difficult to imagine.

In the years leading up to his death, my brother had lost his job as manager of a framing shop, then his partner, and finally, his ability to make art. He'd been a fine draughtsman, with an empathy for others that shone in his methodically rendered portraiture and in the small pencil sketches he'd done of himself. He had a goofy laugh, a ridiculousness that could override his sensitivities, his serious side. He contained multitudes, most of which were never realized.

I never saw him drunk, or even take a drink. This was astonishing, considering the level of his addiction. I have wondered how he did this, when he'd come to stay. On our final Christmas together, it had been just the two of us at my parents' house in Stratford. He was heavier than he'd ever been, but besides that, I wouldn't have said he looked sick—certainly not near death. The next year, he'd planned to come for Christmas dinner, but never arrived. He telephoned me one last time in the spring. I didn't pick up. He spoke to my machine but I can't remember, no matter how I've tried over the years, what he said. A few months after that call, his concerned neighbour telephoned the police, and officers found my brother's body on the floor of his apartment. The counsellor's prediction had come true. He hadn't stopped drinking. He died in September.

There is an art history term for the final stage of work done by artists who died prematurely. Officially, it's called "late-life style" and is defined as "marked changes in the works of creative artists who died young." The artist most often associated with this definition is Jackson Pollock, who died in a car accident when he was in his mid-forties. He was struggling with depression, and alcoholism, near the end, which no doubt affected his work—in terms of both his cognition and his will to make art, which waned in the three years before his death. There is some debate over the authenticity of his purported final work, *Red, Black and Silver*, made in 1956 for his young mistress, the artist Ruth Kligman. She claimed to have watched him paint the work, but in the official records of the artist's estate, the work is "attributed to" Pollock rather than by him, because Kligman, who survived the car accident that killed him, was thought to be an unreliable narrator. Scholars have debated its authenticity for years, but recent evidence suggests Kligman might have been right about *Red, Black and Silver*. The difference between this painting and Pollock's earlier works is clear. Not unlike his friend and peer Willem de Kooning, Pollock's last painting is spare where once he'd filled his canvas. There is an abundance of white space. There are blotches of blue, red, and yellow, but few other colours, and there is playfulness where once there was aggression. It's difficult to find Pollock in this work. It's as if he's already gone.

I have looked for this shift in my brother's late work, some embedded articulation of what was to come, but I have found none. The discernible change in my brother's art was that, in his final years, he stopped creating work at all.

The art that Marsh left behind was divided amongst my father and his remaining children a few months after Marsh died. We gathered one night over the Christmas holidays, at Allyson's home. The house was in the suburbs of Waterloo, set amidst a dizzying twist of roads that led nowhere and then circled back. The street names were variations of one another, most ending or beginning with "Beech," references to the natural world that had been there before the machines plowed the trees, filled in the streams, and poured the concrete streets and cul-de-sacs. My father had arrived bearing all of Marsh's artwork, and my siblings and I helped him prop each drawing, painting, and print against the walls of my sister's house. There were so many works that we ran out of space, and we had to rest some of the art on the stairs leading to the second floor. We chose according to our birth order, which meant I went last. If I could choose again, I'd probably select more serious works. Instead, afraid of what the darker works might reveal, I chose a pencil sketch of a manatee twirling against a Union Jack background; two coloured block prints; a bizarre whipped-cream advertisement that Marsh had done as an assignment for art school; an etching of a kettle; and a geometric lion's face, among other works. My collection of my brother's art went to my parents' house, where it stayed for the next fifteen years while I decamped to one faraway city after another, venturing home for visits but always leaving again, always leaving for someplace farther.

At the time of my brother's death, my father had been working on a series of paintings that he'd started in the mid-sixties, called *My Garden*. These were self-portraits where a small, grey-scale photograph of my dad wandered through otherworldly landscapes that shrieked with colour. He'd posed for the photos, developed them, and then placed his cut-out form into the riotous gardens. In some his image looks back at where he's come from, and in others, he's in the corner sketching, or walking purposefully. In one red landscape, edged with yellow, turquoise threaded through, he sits having a picnic with my mother. Although the photograph might have been taken during their first visit to Europe together, I liked to believe it was during the year we lived in France, when I was a toddler. For several years in my late twenties it hung above the sofa in my apartment. I would look at it and imagine that my three-year-old self was in the bottom-right corner, in a froth of colour that could be the reflection of light and trees on the banks of the Source-Seine. I was there too, just offstage, having fallen into the river, believing I was drowning, in the moments before my parents noticed my absence (maybe as they posed for this self-portrait, the camera on a tripod, the timer ticking) and my father lifted me from the riverbed and restored order to the world.

My father painted only one of the *My Garden* series in 2001, the year my brother died. It is called *My Garden with Reflections*. Each painting in the series has a square bottom that rounds into an arch across the top, and he usually paints both the mat and the frame. This is the only one where the paint strays outside the mat lines, and there is more empty space in this landscape than in the others. Also, in *Reflections*, he looks directly at the camera, arms askance, face blank, one foot pointed out, as if to say, *Now what?* Or, maybe, *What happened?* or *What can I do?* I was accustomed to reading my father's works based on the plot points of his life's narrative — although, mostly, those references were geographic. In *My Garden with Reflections*, though, it was impossible for me to look at the work and think about anything other than my brother's death, wondering, *Now what? What happened? What can I do?*

THE PHOTOGRAPHS THAT I'VE seen of Toronto artist Christiane Pflug are of a young woman. She was never old. She was thirty-six when she died. In these photos she has round eyes, and dark hair parted in the middle. Her voice was high-pitched and childlike, but I might think this because in the recording I heard on a radio documentary, she was play-acting with her two young daughters. They were in their teens when she died by suicide at Hanlan's Point, on Toronto Island, not far from her home. She'd tried before, her husband wrote in a biographical note on a web page devoted to her art, and he listed all the dates and their corresponding geographies: Paris, Wuppertal, Tunis, Toronto, Toronto, then, finally, Toronto. He wrote that it was difficult to stop a suicide bolstered by eighteen years of planning. He used an exclamation point and it seemed the wrong punctuation for a tragedy. An ellipsis, its three dots drifting off into the whiteness of the page, might have been more apt.

Pflug's daughters don't live with their mother's work. She produced only a slim body of paintings and most of these are in public and private collections, so years go by without them seeing their mother's brushstrokes. One daughter, knowing her mother's work, *With the Black Flag*, was on display at the Art Gallery of Ontario, went to visit the painting. It was Pflug's last finished painting, a view from the window of the townhouse the family had rented on Birch Avenue in Toronto. The daughter was alone in the room. Reunited with the painting, she wept freely.

"We can't look at her work without being acutely aware of the loss," she said. I understood exactly what she meant. If Christiane Pflug had lived, she'd be in her eighties now. What she might have achieved, we won't know. Pflug's work is interpreted, so often, through her exit, and so, through a lens of suffering. Her name became synonymous with other talented women artists who died young and by suicide, like Virginia Woolf and Sylvia Plath, who were eulogized, canonized, and fetishized. This chafed at her daughter, who had a different way of looking at this cohort, her mother among them.

"My question is, What could we have done to keep Sylvia and Virginia and my mother alive? What could we have done so that they felt appreciated and strong and valued?" she asked. "Think of how much more incredible work each of them could have given us."

"HE WAS THE MOST talented of all my children," my father said aloud, to no one, although my mother and I were there. He never said this sort of thing. He didn't make proclamations or sweeping statements. He wasn't a terribly dramatic person. We were in the living room of the home in Stratford where my parents had lived since my father's retirement in 2000. My brother had been dead for three days. Dusk gathered outside the windows. I was the only one of my father's children who heard him say this, and, remembering Aidan's paper town, I wasn't sure it was even true. In any case, I didn't care. Who wants to compete with the dead? Besides, I'd already decided I would no longer write. I had gone to school to write about art, but now I knew that art was darkness, and it could be poisonous and frightening, that you could lose your art, your ability to create, to something more demonic and powerful. No matter what, your art could never save you from this force. Even though you turned yourself over to art, it would forsake you, leave, even lead you to your terrible end. Burn down your house, with you inside, calling for help that won't come, doomed.

This disease had passed down to my brother from a different bloodline, but all blood holds an imprint of addiction and my matrilineal line was not spared this defect. I didn't feel immune to slipping into the darkness, to losing my life—but first, my art. Better to let it free before this could happen. I decided I would never write again.

But, years passed, and I couldn't stop writing. In public, these were news articles or small items for fashion or lifestyle magazines, but, in private, in the longer, more difficult work that would take me years to publish, I was writing, specifically, about my brother's death, and, sometimes, about my dad.

In writing about my father in those pages, I had intended to skip over this tragedy. Nearly twenty years had passed, and, besides, I had planned only to talk about the present. But the present encapsulates the past. I could not escape this reliving through writing. I could not spare my father, or myself.

Will I ever stop writing about my brother's death? If I look over my work, this event appears even when not explicit or named. Sometimes it is just a line; other times it is an overt meditation on his loss and how it affected our family in the years that followed. Is writing a radically different act of creation than visual art? If my father's experience lives and breathes in his work, as mine does, then my brother, his loss, has been woven into the products of my dad's imagination in some way.

If this is true, we must all be there, the five children, somewhere in the brushstrokes, my mother, also, and his first wife, his parents as well as his beloved Scottish nursemaid, and his fierce and magical granny who ruled the family funeral home. This is one of the reasons why art of the very old is important, for what it can show us about life and loss across the span of a century in the stretch of a canvas.

CONSIDER AMERICAN ARTIST Alice Neel, at eighty years of age, propped stark naked on a striped wingback chair, blinking defiantly from behind her wide-rimmed old-lady eyeglasses. Sit, for a time, with Neel. Move through the initial shock of seeing an old woman's body and understand the power, inherent. This was 1980. It was the first time an elderly woman had painted herself in the nude. It remains one of the only examples we have, remains radical, even now, forty years on. Her flesh hangs, her nipples point downwards, lines of fat ring her ankles. Her hair is a cloud of white, and there's a fiery rosacea in her pinked cheeks. Her face is partially shadowed in green. The high arch of her brows suggests that you, the viewer, are complicit in this act of self-portraiture. *Are you offended by me?* she asks, and you have to think hard about your answer. She holds a white cloth, and some critics have written this as an act of surrender, but I don't believe it is. It is her painter's rag, part of her arsenal of tools, as necessary to the craft as the paintbrush she holds in her right hand—which is really her left. She was left-handed. She always painted from life. This was a reflection of her image, in a mirror.

Neel painted her most important works in her seventies and eighties, portraits that are tender and stark, many of queer couples, luminaries of Andy Warhol's Factory world. In one portrait, a soft, sweet-eyed man in a rumpled sweater and jeans sits beside his luminescent partner, who is wearing stockings and heels, his lips red like rubies, blue eyeshadow swept over his brow, his crimson hair twisted into ringlets. Neel painted Warhol, too, shirtless, corseted, a zipper of stitches crisscrossing his torso's fleshy middle, scars from an assassination attempt. There is a slight sway to his small but pendulous breasts, the nipples a shock of pink. His eyes are closed, his face alive with surprising colours: sage green, orange, purple, and blue. He is wearing sensible brown trousers and laced-up leather oxfords. He sits on the outline of a sofa, blank, void of colour or detail. No need for filler; the star, Neel knew, and his vulnerability were what we were there to look at.

Neel, whose exacting and heart-stopping portraiture revolutionized this staid, long-standing facet of art into something new, something practically unrecognizable as portraiture, tried, repeatedly, to kill herself over a period of time in her twenties. She'd lost her first child, triggering an emotional collapse and her many suicide attempts. She broke a glass with the intention of swallowing its shards, she tried to asphyxiate herself with a stocking, and she put her head in the oven of her family home. Neel was institutionalized and restrained in a suicide ward, set free only for meals, which she ate with a rubber knife and fork. She was barred from making art and so she painted her fellow patients in secret, and, later, from memory. These were night-wanderers: a woman who'd tried to set herself on fire, another woman who repeatedly beat her head on the floor. "Poor scraps of humanity in grotesque gingham dresses and violety-dun-colored bathrobes," she wrote about her fellow patients. Neel's nude self-portrait, in her eighties, coincided with the height of her career—a solo exhibit at the Whitney, a wildly entertaining turn as Johnny Carson's guest on *The Tonight Show*, and, finally, a feature on the cover of *ARTnews*, the most influential and widely read art magazine in the world. The issue appeared in the month of her death. She was eighty-four years old. What might have been a short life had been lived long.

I RETURNED HOME FIFTEEN years after my brother died. It was the year he would have turned fifty. I'd settled, finally, and bought a house. It was time for me to retrieve the belongings that I'd stored with my parents, including Marsh's art.

My father had constructed a portfolio from two pieces of cardboard to keep the work safe, and he'd written Marsh's name on the outside and, after it, an arrow pointing toward my name. I noticed that the paper had yellowed slightly in a few of the prints, but mostly the work was un-pocked and had no signs of discolouration. Sifting through his art, I remembered the night we'd chosen, one by one, these pieces of our brother's work. Most of it was vaguely familiar, but one drawing I'm certain I didn't choose. It was personal, overly intimate, and I would have been too self-conscious to have drawn it from the rest. It was a 3-by-2-foot self-portrait in pencil of my brother and his former girlfriend, done on paper the colour of concrete. It was untitled, and there was no date and no signature, but he'd been a master renderer, and so both their ages and identities were in the details of the sketch. Still, I don't remember either of them ever looking that fresh, chiselled, or fit. I don't remember my brother's hair being that tidy or his moustache so trim. He had drawn himself with sunglasses on—a disappointment, as I would have liked to have seen his eyes again. This portrait was as realistic as a photograph, but it was also a kind of fantasy. It was as if he'd drawn himself as he hoped to be but wasn't. His former partner, still at his side, with her feathered hair and piercing eyes, appeared more beautiful than I recalled, and he was beautiful, too. They reminded me of film stars from the 1980s. It was warm, wherever those former selves existed; my brother wears a tank top.

I don't know how this work got into the collection of my brother's art that I'd chosen. It's possible that my dad put it there by mistake. But I kept it, regardless, tucked in the portfolio, because I hoped that one day I might manage to hang this piece on a wall, frame it nicely, honour these young people who'd existed long ago, on a day in summer with their entire lives ahead of them, and the end too far off to see, or even imagine.

Raft of the Medusa

AT 23-BY-15-FEET IN ITS gilt frame, *The Raft of the Medusa*, by Théodore Géricault, loomed above my head. I was twenty-four the first time I saw it in person. The makeshift vessel was tilted forward as if I might push myself aboard, the way you do when swimming up to a dock in a lake. My gaze was parallel to the painted corpses with their fishy hue, their bodies providing the sightlines that led up to the living. They formed the base of two triangles, the first leading up through the survivors to the mast, the second to the upright body of a man waving a red flag at a distant ship on the horizon, a speck so small it might be nothing at all. It seemed impossible that the people on board that faraway ship could see the nearly sunken raft, and in reality, it had been a fluke of random marine navigation that saved them. The ship that rescued the final fifteen survivors had chanced upon the raft; it had not been a deliberate rescue mission. The French government had sent no search party their way.

Géricault's raft is an unparalleled work of art, so disturbingly real in its execution that I was nearly sickened by the ocean swell, could smell the rot—and yet, I felt that there was one expression amiss amongst the rest. It was that of an old man, seated in the foreground, left of centre, his head propped on his right fist, his left hand holding the torso of his dead son, keeping the boy's beautiful body, which was perfectly unscarred, from the waves that would inevitably envelope him. I felt the old man looked contemplative, reminiscent of Auguste Rodin's *Thinker*. His face was uncreased. He seemed resigned. His eyes were vacant and searching but he did not, in my opinion, embody the bewilderment of grief, the utter helplessness of a parent facing their dead child. I couldn't see shock's fault line running through his features, one I'd glimpsed only months before. One I couldn't forget. I stood before the painting for a long time, considering the father, puzzling over his expression. He was facing out, facing me, away from the action in the scene, and he seemed unaffected by the hysteria of the other passengers, both their ebullition and despair. He was either oblivious or uncaring about the possibility of rescue. In a work that was a rush of movement, the old man was stiller than the corpses at his feet. For him, all else had fallen away. After a time, I reconsidered. Maybe, I thought, Géricault had got one thing right in the old man's resignation—after facing the tragedy of losing his son, he was beyond saving.

IT WAS IN THE SPRING of 2002 and my brother had been gone two seasons. I'd organized a trip to France with my father. I felt that a journey to the country of his muse might help him heal. After arriving, we spent three days in Paris, staying with my father's friend Guy and his wife, Guillane, who told me that she had trained to be a nun but left the order after reading *Gone with the Wind* while her peers were on a three-day prayer retreat. They lived on the Right Bank in an apartment with soaring windows and a cage-like elevator that fit two people — only if they were slim. By dinner on our first day, I was so exhausted that I fell face-first into my soup bowl and Guillane sent me to bed before serving the main course. The next morning, with my jet lag waning, my father and I visited the Louvre and stayed at the museum until dusk. We set out together, but I tended to drift between works and my father could spend half an hour examining the corner of one oil painting, so we'd often lose track of one another. I'd occasionally circle back and come across him in one of the galleries, and he'd motion me to his side, urging me to look at some small point — a flash of light, a woman's strange facial expression, the movement of colour from one corner to another. "See?" he'd say, showing me something new before we parted ways again.

I'd come upon *The Raft of the Medusa* in a room in the Denon Wing, and was startled to see the real thing, after studying it in university. The raft had a grim but enthralling backstory about a ship that foundered off the west coast of Africa at the onset of the nineteenth century. It was called the *Méduse*, and was part of a fleet heading towards Senegal in 1816 with the intention of reclaiming the colony from the British. There were four hundred people on board, many of them settlers and soldiers, some of them captains and politicians, including the man who'd been slated to become the new governor of Senegal. They had marked the crossing of the equator with an on-board celebration, and during the festivities they ran aground on a sandbar. The captain was an incompetent man of wealth and privilege, a contentious appointment by the French government, and, along with the other elite passengers, he crawled aboard a lifeboat at the first sign of trouble. The ship's carpenter hastily constructed a life raft from lumber stored in the hull for the remaining 150 passengers of lesser rank.

The raft began to sink as soon as they stepped on board. It was initially tied to one of the lifeboats, but the rope either snapped or was intentionally severed within minutes. The people gathered on the raft had no food (save for a bag of ship's biscuits consumed on the first day), and their two casks of fresh water were lost overboard in a fight. Six casks of wine remained as their only sustenance. They were adrift for nearly two weeks. People quickly lost their grasp on rational thought. Many died of starvation; some were murdered. Others, without hope, threw themselves overboard, likely a better choice than remaining on the raft, where passengers had resorted to cannibalism to keep themselves alive.

Géricault approached this painting as a documentarian. He studied the rigidity of corpses in the morgue, sketched the careful fear and resignation of dying patients in hospital, and spent time among the mentally ill in an asylum near his home. He interviewed the two remaining survivors of the raft, gleaning details of their anguish—the rotten smells of the dead, the violence among the living, the powerful thrust of the ocean beneath the sinking raft. All of his research was alive in the work. Both the tragedy and Géricault's painting embarrassed the French government, but it eventually purchased the work, recognizing the painting as a singular shining light, the likes of which spawned an entirely new direction in art. Romanticism was concerned with emotion, human experience, and nature; Géricault wouldn't live to see its ascendance, nor the art that came in the wake of his raft. He was in his late twenties when he finished this painting, and his early thirties when he died of complications following a horse-riding accident.

I WOULD COME TO understand that, with loss, imbalance was a constant state—that there was no forgetting, or overcoming, or getting over loss. Grief was a malleable thing: it grew with you, into different forms and iterations of who you were, but it wasn't a bird to be set free. It had no wings. That year, however, arriving in the city of Lourdes with my father after our stay in Paris, knowing it had provided inspiration for him in the past,

I was hoping for a lift. I knew Lourdes was a place of miracles. It was where the Virgin Mary had appeared in a grotto to a young girl named Bernadette Soubirous, a miller's daughter with dark eyes and a round face who'd been gathering sticks from a nearby river. The "White Lady" requested a chapel, and subsequently, after several more apparitions, a cathedral was built on the site. She encouraged Bernadette to drink from the spring of water that came from the rocks, and soon word spread that the water had curative powers—that it could heal what doctors could not fix.

On that visit with my father, crutches were strung like rows of teeth along the mouth of the grotto. At first, I believed they were the marks of miracles, but, reading more about Lourdes, I realized these were only offerings. There had been just sixty-seven ordained cures since the late nineteenth century when Mary first appeared to Bernadette, and there were hundreds of crutches. Taps extended from the rock face alongside the grotto, and I filled a clear plastic Virgin with holy water and then screwed on her blue-crown lid. My father told me I'd drunk from one of those plastic bottles as a child and I said that seemed a bit sacrilegious.

We walked the hill above the square, following the Stations of the Cross, their golden, life-sized bodies, their blank eyes—no pupils, no irises—the images of Jesus that had imprinted themselves upon me as a toddler. My father stopped to draw while I continued on to the end—the final scene of entombment—before circling back. Seeing the scene as an adult, I understood my childish awe and fear. The lifeless tableaux were violent and sad. What struck me most about my trip to Lourdes as an adult, however, were the streets below, and how they were lined with wheelchair lanes. Instead of the bicycle lanes that I'd seen elsewhere in France, there was a solid red line with a white wheelchair symbol running alongside the sidewalks. This detail, above all, showed the volume of people who were drawn to Lourdes hoping for a cure, to heal, but for whom this fortune never came. Despite this being a place of miracles, the wheelchair lanes suggested something else entirely. For most, there was no cure. After an uncomfortable flight, after days in a hotel, after making an exhausting trek across land and water, they returned unchanged, exactly the same way as they'd arrived. Back then, this depressed me, but I've since come to see it differently. It is only the optimists who undertake such voyages—those who believe in the possibility of a miracle, in the magic of a young girl and a goddess. They must have understood, as they made their way home, that often the healing lies in the journey, rather than the destination.

NOW WE WERE AT a different crossroads, facing another shapeless loss. And, as before, I sought a pilgrimage that might illuminate the path forward. In late August of 2018, I was living at our family cottage by Lake Ontario, and I visited my father at least once a day. It had been a year since his diagnosis, and while dates and days continued to plague him, his creative work had carried on unchanged, as had his social life.

I was in the midst of planning a trip to New York City. There were several shows that seemed suited to the theme of the aging artist and I had a short list of people I hoped to speak with. As my plans progressed, I shared my findings with my father. There was a show on at the Museum of Modern Art called *The Long Run*, about the later arc of artistic careers; the *New Yorker* satirist Bruce McCall had agreed to meet with me. My father would listen, and then tell me stories about his experiences in New York as a young artist. How there was a guy in the corner of a party he attended, someone with long white hair, a strange guy, and he didn't talk to anyone, just stood there silently smoking.

"We all knew it was Andy Warhol," my dad said.

He told me about the New York art dealer in the early sixties who had been interested in his work, but who'd wanted a 40-percent commission. The cut had seemed outrageous to my father. He'd been in the throes of his early career; his art was selling but he hadn't yet managed to find full-time work and he had a rapidly growing family. He passed on the dealer's overture and has since wondered if it might have led to a larger, more international career.

"Why did you say no to him—just because of the money?"

"No," my dad said. "I was arrogant back then."

During one of these conversations, my father fished

his wallet out of his back pocket and began to sift through its contents.

"Here it is," he said, handing me a membership card to the Museum of Modern Art. "Now you won't need to pay the entrance fee."

He'd received the card twelve years ago, when he'd been part of *Transforming Chronologies*, the tectonic-drawing show, at the gallery. He'd travelled there for the opening, and that was the last time he'd visited New York. I thanked him, and slipped the card into my wallet. As I did this, he said, "Just, be sure to get it back to me, okay? Don't lose it."

In that moment, I realized that my father believed he would return to New York and revisit the Museum of Modern Art, and, what's more, that he felt this was possible. I was surprised by his confidence, but I shouldn't have been. He had spent his life travelling for art. He read the weekly *New Yorker* art listings, and he always knew which big shows were blowing through the city. His thinking seemed nearly delusional, and yet, it was also reassuring that he saw his life as unchanged. Because, in the way it mattered most — the way he perceived his life — it *was* unchanged: he remained the same person.

IN AN ESSAY PUBLISHED in his posthumously gathered writing, *Everything in Its Place: First Loves and Last Tales*, Oliver Sacks wrote that telling a patient about their diagnosis can be fraught, but that ultimately people want to know the truth, however grim the prospects. This becomes somewhat more complex for patients facing dementia, Sacks says, which not only infers that death is near, if not imminent, but also that mental decline is inevitable. Most troubling to the patients, he writes, is the perceived "loss of self."

Sacks goes on to describe two different cases. In the first, a doctor with Alzheimer's disease became a patient in the very hospital he once ran. The doctor assumed that he was still working, and that his role was unchanged — overseer, medical professional. Sometimes, under lax supervision, he would peruse the medical charts of active patients, once coming across his own. Reading his diagnosis, the doctor immediately understood what he faced. "God help me," he said, and wept. Still, for the most part, reassuming his role as doctor, or at least perceiving that he remained in this role, had a positive impact on the doctor's sense of self. Similarly, Sacks writes of a man with dementia who'd worked as a boarding school janitor for most of his career. Now ensconced in a care home, a living arrangement that was not unlike his previous place of work, he carried on his custodial duties undeterred, checking that the kitchen appliances were cleaned and operating properly, the windows locked at night, the furnace running well, and the laundry room tidily in order.

Sacks asks: Should we tell the doctor that he is not really a doctor, or the janitor that he is no longer a janitor? "It seemed not only pointless but cruel to do so — and might well have hastened his decline."

Based on these cases, it seemed that, rather than a loss of self, there could be a continuum, and that in some form, our identities—the roles we carry, the deep ruts that we have worn into the terrain of our memories—might remain.

After hearing the geriatrician's diagnosis, I'd been nervous to see my dad the first time. I knew it was ridiculous, but I couldn't shake the feeling that he'd be somehow changed, immediately, by this new way of being, a different person than the one I'd seen last. My sister, Robin, saw him first, and had confessed to having had similar thoughts. "But he's just my same old dad," she said. On the surface this was a simple conclusion, and yet the stigma of dementia is profound, and few people can reach the same level of thought as my sister had. Even specialists in the field of dementia research face barriers. Recently, I'd met with Dr. Sherry Dupuis at the University of Waterloo to discuss her research and programming, which uses the arts to advocate and educate on dementia, and which regularly draws on interviews and uses input from people who have dementia. She first began interviewing people with dementia in the 1990s, after finishing her undergraduate program in music and while working towards a master's degree in gerontology.

"People thought I was nuts," she said, referring to those interviews. "No one did that."

Even twenty years later, the backlash is relentless. At a recent conference, a fellow academic challenged her following a talk she gave that included several direct quotes from interviews with people who had dementia.

"He said, 'You have made those quotes up,'" she told me. "'There is no way that people with dementia could speak that eloquently.'"

"Are you calling me a fraud?" she'd asked him. "What are you saying?"

Sitting across from her in a busy Starbucks at the university, the chatter of students rising around us, I could sense her fatigue, her exhaustion in fighting this stigma, but I also sensed her resolve. Her first job after university had been in a care home where many of the residents had dementia. She loved them. A talented musician, she played music with the residents, watching people who'd been fairly non-responsive, without communication, revive to a song, even sing the words along with her. The words were there, layered into the experience of a life—maybe early, maybe mid-life—but there, forever, nonetheless, always.

The fundamental misunderstanding of our time— maybe of all time—is that we belong to one age group or another. The idea that seniors, or the elderly, or old people—whatever it makes us feel better to call them— are anyone other than ourselves in a few scant decades is a farce. Barring illness or injury, we will all grow old. There is no "us" and "them." There was only ever an us. In her brutal rumination on aging, *The Coming of Age*, Simone de Beauvoir wrote that "old age is particularly difficult to assume because we have always regarded it as something alien, a foreign species: 'Can I have become a different being while I still remain myself?'"

The answer to her question is: no.

The answer to her question is, also: yes.

IN HIS FINAL DECADE, my maternal grandfather kept his prospector's equipment—including his canvas rucksack, a tent, a miner's headlamp, and his pickaxe—packed up neatly in the attic of his home, believing that one day he'd return to the bush. Even when Parkinson's disease made him shake and he could barely eat, he would inquire after his backwoods gear. It was a large part of his identity. He'd been most at home outside, in nature. In old age he kept waiting for a journey north that would never come, and the tools and necessities of his early prospecting life stayed in the attic, unused, until he died. What, I wonder, might have happened if someone had taken him for one final voyage to the vast landscape he'd explored throughout his career? They'd have needed to adapt the trip. No sleeping on the floor of a canvas tent; more passive viewing than bushwhacking. We'll never know. It was too extreme an idea. But, New York? Well, anything is possible there.

The night after my dad gave me his card, I looked up the Warwick, the 1920s Midtown hotel that sits opposite the Museum of Modern Art where I knew he would want to stay. My eyes watered at the prices. I'd planned to pitch up in some careworn vacation rental on the outskirts of the city—bearing the foibles and bathroom habits of whoever hosted me for the lowest price. I checked the timing of flights, and even searched the internet for other people who'd considered travelling with an elderly parent to New York City. A thread on a travel site was divisive. Some claimed it was the perfect place for seniors, and others warned against exhausting older relatives by foisting this kind of trip on them. "Who is this experience for?" one commenter asked. "You, or your parent?"

I wavered, knowing that my father was healthy but, also, understanding that he'd recently turned eighty-four. Then I thought of my grandfather's camping equipment and how the thought of returning to his beloved wilderness had sustained him during his final years.

The next day I found my dad in his drawing room and I handed him his MoMA card. I told him he'd need it, and asked if he'd join me on my trip to New York.

"Yes," he said, his eyes brightening. "Yes, of course I'd like to go to New York with you."

And, just like that, we were travelling companions again.

Articulated Lair

W E KNEW BY OUR first night in New York that
my father had forgotten his cell phone at home.
My mother had insisted that it should be the only item
my father remembered, besides his passport, which
she'd handed to me at the airport in Toronto for safe-
keeping. He hadn't protested. That kind of care never
bothered him. He liked it when women looked after the
details. When we arrived at our suite at the Warwick,
I'd searched his luggage, unzipped every pouch, shaken
out all the clothes that my mother had folded neatly
into place, and looked through the pockets of his suit
jacket—but there was no cell phone. I told him that
he'd forgotten his phone at home, and that this would
be our secret. He'd laughed, agreeing to stay silent on
the matter. He was a good secret-keeper by then. He
wouldn't remember that we'd searched for the phone,
and that it hadn't turned up.

Here is what he did remember to pack in his suitcase: two fountain pens (he never drew in pencil), six
felt-tipped markers, and a portfolio, about the size
of a paperback novel, made from two pieces of cardboard fastened together with silver duct tape. It held
a modest stack of thick, handmade paper, each sheet
frayed at the edges—ripped rather than cut because
scissors made the lines too uniform, too sharp and
unnatural. The phone was meaningless to him, but
the art supplies were a necessity of life.

At first, the trip to New York felt like an escape. It
was a wormhole that we fell through into a fantasy of
immortality. That night, we went to an opening for a
group show where all the artists were old. No artist
under the age of sixty was allowed to show their work
in this space. Called the Carter Burden Gallery, it was
housed in a former factory building in Chelsea. The
crowd was wrinkled and bright-eyed. The noise of the
party hit us like a wall as soon as the elevator doors
opened. It reminded me of my father's art openings in
the eighties, nineties, and early aughts, ones that had
taken place in old brick warehouses not unlike this one,
where the pipes and wiring were exposed along the ceilings and the wooden floors creaked underfoot.

The difference tonight was that the artists in the gallery were greying into their final years. It was a version
of the future, or maybe the present. The largest cohort
in the history of the world was growing old at exactly
the moment in time when humans were living longer
than ever before. We hesitated at the entrance, standing

on the fringes of a new frontier, one that seemed like a promise. It felt as if each one of those artists stood on the edge of possibility, on the cusp of being discovered.

Once in the show space, my father followed a series of hinged, door-like wood-and-steel sculptures as if they were breadcrumbs, until he discovered the artist, Jay Moss, a ninety-six-year-old World War Two vet, sitting against a far wall, one arm resting on a walker. The artist's son approached us and introduced himself. He was eager, and proud. He told us that his father's work was influenced by his experiences in the Second World War. First-hand accounts of our last global battle were etched, hammered, moulded, and marked into these sculptures. Later, in a *New York Times* article, I read that Moss had been drafted after high school, had served in Europe, and had been evacuated with trench foot, pneumonia, and malaria. He'd seen a truckload of American bodies coming back from the front and, noticing their hand-knitted caps — "like the ones we all wore under our helmets" — he'd thought of his mother. It had been unbearable. After the war, he became a designer. First, he made theatre sets, and later, he made lamps, but at night he worked on his sculptures in his basement studio, making art only for himself. He'd started showing his work in his nineties. For most of his life, he'd been afraid of rejection, feeling it would be too painful — maybe because his work was influenced by the darkest period of his life.

In an article he'd written on his father's first show, Moss's son had asked him if he was at all glad for having been a soldier in the war, knowing how it would shape the artist he'd become.

His father had been surprised by the question. His eyes had widened.

"Fuck no."

In the gallery, my father bent down to shake Moss's hand and they had a brief conversation that was lost in the din of the crowd. It was rare for my father to meet artists a decade his senior these days.

"He had a face like El Greco," my father said as we left, referring to the sixteenth-century Spanish artist. "Very long and thin, very sophisticated."

We ate dinner past nine that night, an hour that seemed outrageously late. My father worried over the menu. The server returned three times before I gently tugged the laminated sheet from my father's hand and ordered for him. He'd been up before five a.m. that morning, anxious about the trip. He'd then been hauled across airports and cities. He was eighty-four years old and tired, and yet, undeterred. He ordered a bottle of red wine, which we easily finished, and then he ordered a towering slice of chocolate cake for dessert and ate the entire thing.

On our way home we inched across the city in a taxi, the little televisions embedded in the backs of the front seats repeatedly telling us the story of a woman who crocheted tiny replica dolls of Ruth Bader Ginsburg. My father watched the city slip by, sometimes finding it recognizable and other times in awe at how it had changed. We drove through Times Square, which was apocalyptic with its giant concrete barriers to prevent terrorist-manned vehicles from mowing through the crowds. The people seemed unaware of lurking danger. Their faces, tilted upwards, were lit purple, blue, and yellow by the towering flashing signs, the tickertape spelling disaster, the ads selling dreams.

The next morning, over breakfast, we spoke of the elderly sculptor we'd met at the art show.

"You said he looked like El Greco."

"Oh, did I?" my dad said. "Well, then, he probably did."

THE DAY BEFORE, AT the airport, my dad had remembered there was a shoeshine station at the foot of an elevator in the departure lounge, and sure enough, the doors had opened on the ground floor to reveal an old-fashioned set-up with elevated wooden seats and several men in white shirts attending to the footwear of the various airline passengers. My father climbed into place, wearing his grey suit coat and tan pants, his green glasses hanging from the string around his neck, looking every bit the distinguished senior that he was. There was a woman sitting to his right, probably nearing sixty, with short, spiky red hair, her glasses a riot of colour encircling large, green eyes rimmed in dark pencil. She leaned toward my father.

"Where are y'all from?" she asked, in a drawl so thick it seemed as if she were exaggerating for effect.

My father smiled pleasantly, but did not answer.

He looked down to where I was standing, extended his arm, as if presenting me as his response. I hadn't experienced this before. I was suddenly nervous, as if I also might forget where my father lived, or somehow get the answer wrong.

"East of Toronto," I answered, and my father nodded, smiling back at the woman.

"That's right," he said.

And yet he remained sharp, he was good company, and he made me laugh. We began our second day at the Museum of Modern Art, first visiting a retrospective of work done by the conceptual artist Bruce Nauman.

We stood beside each other, reading the curatorial statement that said the artist had spent "half a century inventing forms to convey both the moral hazards and the thrill of being alive."

My dad rolled his eyes.

"*Ploppa del toro*," he said, using his preferred Spanish-themed neologism, a phrase I'd heard him say all of my life.

My dad's mind might occasionally stumble, but he still knew what was bullshit and what was real.

From there we moved on to *The Long Run*, the group show compiled from the MoMA collection that considered the arc of an artist's career. Many of the works showcased had been done later in life. The first work we saw was an installation by the French-born, U.S.-based artist Louise Bourgeois, whose 1982 retrospective at MoMA had marked her first solo show, at the age of seventy-one. *Articulated Lair*, 1986, was the first in what would become a series of installations Bourgeois called "cells." In this one, accordioned walls, about seven feet tall, surrounded a space large enough for four or five people. The exterior was painted black, and you entered through an open door under an arched doorway, which could be shut — although the viewer was not encouraged to touch the artwork, as with my father's sculptures. A child-sized black stool sat in the interior of the piece, and dark, bulbous shapes hung from strings along the walls of the cell, like hanging meat in a butcher's shop, or blackened human organs. A lair, Bourgeois felt, could be a place of refuge and safety, and yet, it was also a place one could be lured into and trapped. I felt more trapped than safe as my father and I shuffled through the space. The walls brought to mind the folding partitions found in church basements and funeral parlours. Structurally, the work was impressive, all the more so because Bourgeois was seventy-five when she executed the piece, which would have required not only the physical strength, but also the artistic confidence to carry out a work of this scale. Further, this piece marked the beginning, not the denouement, of a new direction in her career, a period that followed the arrival of the critical reception and interest that had eluded her for most of her working life. It was this distance from the art world that buoyed her practice. "For many years, fortunately, my works were not sold for profit or for any other reason," she said. "My image remained my own, and I am very grateful for that. I worked in peace for forty years."

There was a recent trend for older women artists, like Bourgeois, to be fêted after a life spent making art in relative obscurity — some had died by the time their veil was lifted and others were elderly, although not always cognizant. Cuban-born American artist Carmen Herrera was 101 when she had her first solo show at the Whitney, and was in her late eighties when she sold her first painting. These women artists were connected to historic art movements, as with Saloua Choucair, the Lebanese artist whose solo show at the Tate Modern marked her international debut at age ninety-seven. Both Choucair and Bourgeois had studied under the cubist artist Fernand Léger in Paris in the 1930s and '40s, and this provided pedigree and a direct connection to a documented period of art, now vanished. Unlike with young art stars, collectors were able to peruse the arc of an entire career in the cases of these women artists. Also, their work was less expensive than that of their male counterparts. In terms of investments, old-women artists had become a sure bet.

At the same time, curators were attempting to address gaps in the collections of their institutions. They couldn't change the past — the dealers who wouldn't show Herrera's large-scale geometric paintings because she was a woman, or the fact that Choucair was born into Lebanese society at a time that saw women's artistic ambitions as dangerous and in need of suppression.

It was these struggles, too, that collectors and curators actively sought in the work of old-women artists. "These women understand the frailty of their success," said Frances Morris, the Tate Modern's first female director and a champion of work, often by women, that has traditionally fallen outside the canon. "It makes them more innovative in their later careers and keeps their work young."

Headlines in newspapers and in art magazines rewrote their futures, however short: "Why Old Women Have Replaced Young Men as the Art World's Darlings"; "The Rise of the Older Woman Artist"; and "Miraculous Resurrections: the Contemporary Art Market of Older or Deceased Women Artists."

This was delightful, and gratifying, but there was a troubling undercurrent, a rewriting of history at play. An article in the *Telegraph* suggested that the seventy-seven-year-old British artist Rose Wylie had "tried her hand" at painting after raising her family; yet a deeper probe into Wylie's biography turns up a full life in art, starting with several years at the Dover School of Art in her twenties. Wylie's large-scale works are alive with ambiguously human and animal shapes, and coded with deceptively simple prose — *WILL I WIN* runs like ticker-tape beneath a bulbous, stretched figure skater. Her works are cartoonish and yet not for a child's room, as with her *Red Painting: Bird, Lemur & Elephant*, where the giant red animals look like they're part of a crime scene. A slew of major solo exhibits followed her re-entry into the art world in her late seventies, "well past the regular age of retirement," as one newspaper writer quipped.

Of her commercial success, Wylie was quoted in a 2012 article in the *Guardian* saying that she and her husband, the artist Roy Oxlade, had decided that he would concentrate on his career and she would bring up the children. Their family depended on his teaching salary—which was also the case with my own parents and most of the artist couples of my father's generation. My father taught art at the University of Waterloo; his friend Hugh Mackenzie at the Ontario College of Art; and Roy Oxlade at summer schools in Kent. Wylie went on to say that, as a couple, she and her husband decided "it was not a good idea for two parents to paint, because painting is very isolating and you do tend to focus on yourself and children then become an irritation. I don't think it works, and I think the bringing up of children is hugely important. So I brought up the children and I think that was a good idea."

My father was a man of Oxlade's generation, and, unusually, for a period of time in the seventies he was a single parent to my two sisters. He'd accepted this role, but he'd also sought a way out.

"Don't think for a minute that someone as benign as your father wasn't looking for an opportunity to find someone to look after his children," my mother has said to me. At the end of their first trip to Europe together, as the weight of her grief was slowly lifting, my father said to my mother, "You seem like the kind of person with whom I could travel with the children."

Under my father's watch, and no doubt rooted in the troubled demise of their parents' marriage and their mother's alcoholism, my teenaged sisters were untethered and wild. They couldn't even fake good behaviour. They simply wouldn't have known how. They were foul-mouthed and feral, their fights legendary. Once, while staying at a hotel in France, one sister locked the other in a wardrobe—along with the teenaged bellhop—and then left the building. As a child I begged to hear this story at bedtime. I loved to imagine the silence in the darkened wardrobe, my oldest sister shoulder-to-shoulder with the young bellhop, a complete stranger, while my other sister wandered the cobblestone streets of some charming French village, the weight of the key in her pocket. Years later, long after my two sisters had grown into adulthood and I was nearly a teenager, my mother began to occasionally travel to attend literary events. Once, when I was twelve, she'd been out of the country for a number of days on a book tour. She called my father from the airport when she returned home, and asked after me.

"Emily," my father said, pausing for a beat. "I haven't seen her in a while."

Perhaps it was these kinds of scenarios that Wylie aimed to avoid by taking on the bulk of the childcare. Or, maybe there was something deeper going on in the lives of two artists—not a rivalry, necessarily, but something unspoken between a man and a woman, about whose career was more important, whose time and work needed more tending, attention, and care. My father's singular focus on art meant that he never learned to cook, that yardwork languished, and that children under his watch tended to run free, and this left the more emotional labour of the household to my mother—knowing who my friends were, organizing lessons, picking me and a friend up from a sleepover and smelling the whiff of alcohol evaporating from our bodies, questioning me afterwards, grounding me for my transgressions. The domestic realm was a space my father rarely entered. This wasn't a refusal on his part; it was more of a passive evasion.

My parents could not be true rivals, as Wylie and Oxlade might have been, as they never strayed into each other's art. My father held a reverence for litera-ture; likewise, my mother for visual art—she'd even majored in art history at university. But neither crossed the boundary into the other's craft. I asked my mother, once, if my father had ever felt diminished by her suc-cess. She was adamant in her response.

"No," she said. "He's always been very proud of me."

I gathered, also, that he'd enjoyed the travel perks when she was published in Europe—and the three-course meals at literary awards.

"What if you'd been an artist?"

She considered the question, but not for long.

"I don't think it would have worked as well."

Wylie, Choucair, Herrera, and Bourgeois were not late bloomers; they simply worked and lived long enough to see a shift in what and who the art-world gate-keepers considered to be an artist. A woman didn't give up art to raise her family, she didn't "try her hand" at painting after bringing up her children. It was, instead, that art happened in and around her home, her lair. For me, this struggle between the domestic and the public was the central tension of *Articulated Lair,* the sculpture by Bourgeois. There is a particularly feminine conflict in making the choice to stay or to leave, and there is danger inherent in both decisions.

MY FATHER'S PACE HAD slowed. I would turn around in the gallery and find he was not at my side. I'd retrace my route, a tic of panic in my step, until I found him, sometimes two rooms back. He'd always been slow in art galleries, but now he was barely moving. His blue eyes were watery with fatigue. He was quiet. I suggested we return to the hotel, but he resisted.

"You go, I'll follow."

But I couldn't leave without him. The fantasy of immortality that I'd engaged in the previous night, when I'd photographed our reflection in the mirror above the restaurant's bar—the glass dusky and dim, and the candlelight, glassware, and bowl with peeled lemon making it seem as if we were onlookers in a Flemish still life—had faded. Although the photo, grainy and soft, could have been taken twenty years ago, it wasn't.

I couldn't leave my father to find his way back to the hotel alone. We both knew he would come with me, but we had to discuss the possibility before he'd relent. It would become a new ritual.

"We can come back tomorrow," I said.

"It's fine, you go," he said.

"We've only got the one hotel key," I said. This was

the final piece of information that he needed, that would push the moment forward.

"Oh, well, in that case, I'll go with you," he said. "We'll come back another day."

Starry Night(s)

THE NEXT MORNING, ON our way back to the Museum of Modern Art, we walked behind a father and daughter as we approached the entrance. He was wearing a woollen overcoat and shiny brown shoes. He looked a little old-fashioned, proper. She was wearing woollen tights decorated with tiny hearts, an emerald-green velvet jacket, and a corduroy dress. Her hair was pulled neatly into two braids that hung down her back, each fastened with a bow. They paused at the entrance and the father bent down to his little girl, put his arm around her and pointed upwards to the entrance sign above them, letting her know that they'd arrived. My father looked at me and nodded towards them, and I felt that in his gesture he was saying, *That was us, in the past.* But, then, he pointed at the little girl and said my daughter's name—so, in this small tableau in which I saw the past, he saw the present, and maybe even the future.

It was Saturday, which meant that MoMA was brutal with crowds. In the second-floor gallery space showcasing European art from the nineteenth and twentieth centuries, there was a crush of tourists. I was anxious as I steered my father through the visitors. He was slow-paced in the thick of the crowd, as if he were moving through water, and I grew frustrated by the waves of people and their indifference to his slowness, how they pushed past, jostling him in their wake, how they tugged their friends along in a line like a riptide.

My father saw ghosts in the gallery that day. He pointed to an older woman, her wiry hair swept into a bun on the top of her head. "Look, Em," he said. "Dot Mackenzie." Dot had been dead for some years by then. In the departure lounge at the airport in Toronto, he'd pointed out a man whose balding, sloped head was identical to that of his brother David, who'd died nearly five years before. Now my father addressed the dead artists, the other ghosts in the gallery — Cézanne, Picasso, Van Gogh — as if they were peers in the art scene, as if he'd known them personally, because, in a way, he had. He had studied their marks and approached an understanding of their now long-ago decisions. He'd known their art intimately, and, in this way, he'd known them, also.

My father's friends were a mix of the living and the dead, and so, too, were his family members. He was the only living person who could bring scenes from his childhood, growing up in a funeral home, to memory, because he was the only one among that cast of characters still alive. His granny, his nurse, the cook, his parents, and, a few years before, his brother, had all left the world. But this hadn't severed my father's relationship to them. He'd lived long enough that the line between the underworld and the living had grown fainter for him than it was for people a few generations younger. As Mavis Gallant wrote in perhaps the most autobiographical story of her canon, "Voices Lost in Snow": "...the only authentic voices I have belong to the dead."

Earlier that fall I'd met John Moffat, a physicist in his eighties who was still working out of his office at the Perimeter Institute in Waterloo, a leading centre for research and education in foundational theoretical physics. Moffat was identified as brilliant from childhood, and as a young adult he'd started a correspondence with Einstein that lasted several years. In his ninth decade, he'd continued to publish papers, hundreds per year, and his blackboard was engulfed in the kinds of scribbles that you'd associate with the creative mind of a scientist on the brink of discovery. We'd met so that we might discuss just that—the continued spark, into old age—and, as with my father, I gently prodded him into the present, asking questions about his current life, his days, what they looked like, how they unfolded, his breakthroughs, now, and how they were different, and also how they were the same as those of the past.

He'd obliged, and yet, I soon realized, it was impossible to ask someone to speak about their present without acknowledging their past, which he did by going back to his childhood during the Second World War. He began to describe how he'd been taken from his parents, for safety, and he was overcome with sorrow. Tears ran down his face and I was sorry for having brought this up for him, and said so, but he waved my comment away. He told me that he continued to suffer from post-traumatic stress disorder from his experiences in the war. This was how the stress manifested, he said: with tears. I realized, sitting in his office, almost painfully modern in its sharp angles, its glass-and-steel beauty, that he was both living now and living then, and that the past was not history, but alive, in the present, as he continued to re-experience these traumas. He could not escape his childhood, his past, even in his elder-hood, because it remained alive, for him, as it did for my father, as it does for us all.

IN THE EUROPEAN GALLERY at MoMA, I leaned over to my father, my hand on his arm, a protective measure against the movement of the crowd.

"There seem to be quite a lot of art lovers here today."

"Really?" he asked, and he raised his eyebrows as he turned to look at the densely populated gallery. "How many of the art lovers are looking at the art?"

He was right. They were collecting the art, taking photographs and selfies with their smartphones. Would they truly look at these images later, I wondered—pore over them in the quiet of their hotel room, on the air-plane flying home, in their houses or university dorms?

Maybe they would post an image to social media, one of the endless selfies that, earlier that day, I'd seen taken in front of Picasso's *Les Demoiselles d'Avignon*, as people stood, not looking at the painting, but with their backs to the work, smiling into the cameras on their smartphones as the angular nudes looked on impassively, as they'd done for the century that they've been on display there. I'd seen Van Gogh's *The Starry Night* in multitudes as hands lifted tiny screens to capture the celebrity painting. I had not managed an unobstructed view of the real thing.

There have always been gallery crowds in my lifetime, though perhaps not on my father's early trips to Europe. I'd visited Florence as a teenager, and the line for entrance into the Uffizi Gallery had wrapped around three city blocks. But this urge to insert ourselves into the art, to capture it, to display our experience rather than inhabit the moment, had a lurid, disturbing feel for me.

I knew my feelings were old-fashioned. I wasn't looking to the future, I was experiencing a tipping point in the present: the moment when the way humans looked at art changed. If I were being generous, I might accept that we have found new ways of seeing, of interacting with art, which, on some level, are more meaningful: each person — positioning themselves, tidying their hair, and angling their chin to avoid rolls — is experiencing the work with the physicality of their body, arranging themselves within frames of their own making, taking ownership of the art. Maybe I could see how the kaleidoscope of Starry Nights was beautiful, how it was a masterwork reinterpreted for the modern age—although for me, all those tiny screen versions, even together, could never achieve the inherent wonder, the mysterious power, of the original. Mostly, however, I felt that, as we stood before the most recognized painting in all of art history, it had been transmuted and obscured and fragmented into hundreds of tiny versions of itself—so shattered that I was no longer sure of what the original looked like.

I'd seen this happen before—not to a work of art, but to a town my father had once loved. I was twenty-two, and we were travelling together through Spain and the South of France. My father had wanted to show me the town of Lloret de Mar, on the northern coast of Spain, where he'd lived over a winter in the 1960s with his first wife and my two sisters, before my brothers were born. He told me how Allyson, at four, had gone to the local school and worn a grey smock over her clothing, as all Spanish schoolchildren did. Robin, who was one, had stayed home with her mother. It was a fishing village, and tiny boats had dotted the shoreline and lain in the sun on stretches of yellow sand.

We'd started our trip in the mountains, spending several days in Ronda, one of my father's pilgrimage sites, a mountaintop town connected by soaring aqueducts. The birds in Ronda fly beneath you, as if the world were inverted and the sky was below the earth. Our hotel was built into the side of the gorge and had steel bars on the balcony so that tourists couldn't inadvertently, or intentionally, fall into the chasm. There were also

bars on the windows of the terrace where we ate breakfast, watching the honey buzzards and rock sparrows
swoop and soar below us. From Ronda we travelled to
Madrid, to see a retrospective of work by the Spanish
artist Antoni Tàpies at the Prado, and later, en route
from Barcelona to Figueres, we stopped in the small
town of my father's past.

I was asleep when we arrived in Lloret de Mar,
having been carsick earlier. I awoke as we were driving
down a hill towards a bank of hotels that were strung
along the shore, mostly obscuring the view of the
ocean. It did not look like a fishing village. I could not
see a beach. There were no small wooden boats. Nearly
four decades had passed since 1964, when my father had
lived in this small Spanish town by the sea, before the
birth of mass tourism, budget airlines, holiday homes,
and global hotel chains. The streets he'd known had
been relatively empty then, but were now busy with
cars and scooters. It was unrecognizable to him. He
wasn't able to navigate through the town, as there were
no remembered landmarks for him. The world of his
past, of his memory, had disappeared. In 2000, Lloret de
Mar was a maze of one-way streets and my father grew
visibly frustrated, turning around in narrow laneways
thick with parked cars, as he tried to find his way. He
was looking for a town that no longer existed, a town
of ghosts, and it was as if he were a ghost also, as were
my sisters, and their mother—people who belonged
to a different era. I felt like an interloper. I belonged to
this new world, the world of soaring hotel blocks and

tourist shops, but not to the old one, the better world, the one that he longed for. We didn't end up stopping in the town, although we'd planned to park the car and take a walk to see his former apartment, as well as my sister's old primary school, and then to eat lunch at a small beachside café. Instead, with some difficulty, my father found his way back to the highway and we left the new, unrecognizable town of the future behind.

"It doesn't matter," he said, when he'd regained some clarity of thought. "There was nothing there to see now. It's all gone."

The day before, in Barcelona, we'd seen the Sagrada Familia, Catalan architect Antoni Gaudí's cathedral born of a fever dream. It was centuries into its construction, and still, as we walked the perimeter, much of it remained under scaffolding, in ongoing progress as the workmen of the day carried out the vision of a long-dead artist, knowing that there were workers before them who'd toiled on this same monument and that there would be workers who would continue their own efforts when they grew tired and old, and even after they died. It was constantly in flux and always the same, flouting the passage of time and also obeying its dictum.

Our final stop was Arles, France. This is where our paths would diverge. My father planned to head north to Paris and then fly home, and I would continue eastwards to Nice, where I'd attended school as a teenager. My plans were ambiguous, but I was young enough not to care. I knew I'd find work, as I'd done before — cleaning some youth hostel or hotel, working under the table for room and board—and that this could sustain me. I had a return plane ticket to Canada in six months' time.

In Arles, we stayed in a small hotel in the city centre, a view of the Rhône from the balcony. During our last meal together—dinner at a restaurant a few blocks from our hotel—my father became sentimental and said I reminded him of his mother, who'd been dead a decade by then, for her mild manner and her kindness. I puzzled over this, as I wasn't sure my personality warranted this comparison; also, it was a quiet compliment. I'd have preferred to embody his fiery granny, the matriarch of the funeral home, the fierce defender of his early career. I don't think either comparison was entirely apt, but the truth is that I was still forming then, and hadn't yet grown into the woman I'd become—who is, I think now, a bit of both grandmothers, and, also, neither of them, because she is her own self.

On our last night in the South of France, twenty years ago now, we walked back to our hotel along the bank of the Rhône, the curve of the bay stretching out before us. The street lamps, hanging from spiral-topped poles that dotted the riverside walk, reflected across the water, just as they reflected on the water in Van Gogh's other Starry Night painting, the one he'd made a few months before the more famous work. This earlier work, *Starry Night over the Rhône*, was an evening scene of Arles as seen from across the bay, which was the scene before us that night. Van Gogh described the painting, in a letter to his brother, Theo, as "tranquil." This was the opposite to *The Starry Night,* always described by art critics as roiling, tempestuous, and charged with energy. Vincent told Theo that if he could achieve this tranquility in all of his works, he'd sell more paintings. He wouldn't have to worry so much about money. He'd enclosed a sketch of *Starry Night over the Rhône* and described its colours — the water was royal blue, the ground was mauve, the Great Bear constellation, seen in the stars of an aquamarine sky, was "a sparkling green and pink, whose discreet paleness contrasts with the brutal gold of the gas."

My father reminded me of this work as we stood on the bank of the river after dinner that night, pointing across the water to the twinkling lights. It seemed in that moment that we were at the very angle where the artist had first sketched the scene. Van Gogh's time in Arles was sorrow-filled, and searching. He painted the night sky, as he wrote in another letter to Theo, to quell some deep yearning for spirituality that he could not grasp in life. He died by a self-inflicted gunshot wound two years after writing those words.

I'd seen *Starry Night on the Rhône* four years before, in Paris, at the Musée d'Orsay, and, remembering the painting, I understood that it was an imagined version of the townscape and water before us — not a mirror image or even a likeness, but, instead, the artist's emotional transcendence of the harbour's gas lamps as their light danced across the water with the shimmer of stars overhead. Still, as I walked along the bank of the river with my father — me at twenty-two, him at sixty-five — I could almost see the vision that had inspired Van Gogh to paint his work more than a century before. Almost. The scene was not identical to the scene of the past. Time changes landscapes: it had changed, drastically, the small Spanish fishing village of Lloret de Mar; it had also, with a lighter touch, changed the night vista across the Rhône. In the years since Van Gogh had painted this scene, the lights, now electric and many, had lit the city to the point that it shone — windows were aglow, lights lined the streets. A secondary effect, unintended but drastic, was that this brightness had also illuminated the night sky, obscuring the stars. I could not see a single one.

The Runner

O**N THE SATURDAY AFTERNOON** of our New York
trip, I left my father in our hotel room to visit
with the artist and writer Bruce McCall. It was a conundrum. I'd planned this visit for months, and yet it was
only in the day leading up to it that I'd come to understand the risk of leaving my father alone. I travelled to
McCall's Upper West Side apartment feeling panicked,
imagining my father reaching for the doorknob of our
room, exiting, riding the elevator down to the lobby and
then walking towards the revolving doors that would
whoosh him into the mouth of the city. What he might
do next, I couldn't envision. My mind would go dark
for a moment before the reel restarted. It played on a
loop: the doorknob, the elevator, the revolving door.

Before leaving, I'd retrieved my dad's art supplies
from his luggage, which was a modest-sized carry-on.
On past trips he'd carried oversized and overweight

suitcases filled with art catalogues, portfolios of loose paper, drawings-in-progress, oil paints, rags, paintbrushes, pots of ink, and fountain pens. The suitcases were always black and boxy and painted, on all six sides, with a large, white "U," distinguishing them from their lookalikes on the luggage carousels. My father was zealous about personalizing his baggage, and occasionally I'd come home with a new suitcase, stay for a holiday, maybe just a weekend, and by the time I was packing to leave, my luggage would be forever branded with a large, white "U" on each side.

From my father's supplies, I chose a few sheets of paper, several pens, and some markers and pencil crayons, and laid them on the table of the roll-top bureau in our hotel suite. I hoped that he'd find them after waking from a nap and spend the remaining hours alone drawing, removing any temptation to leave the room while I was out.

On my way to meet McCall, I walked along a stretch of Sixth Avenue that had transformed into a pedestrian-only market selling Guatemalan handicrafts, framed black-and-white photographs of the Empire State Building and the Statue of Liberty, *I Love NY* T-shirts, and piles of cheap coloured beads. Beneath the city I rattled north on the Broadway–Seventh Avenue line, sitting under a stretch of self-help ads that wrapped the interior of the car, and then surfaced in the spartan pomp of Park Avenue, walking the final stretch along the eastern wall of Central Park. It was, I realized, as if I'd wandered through a series of McCall's *New Yorker* covers.

"I've lived in Manhattan for forty-odd years, and urban life throws out countless humor possibilities," he said in a 2018 interview with his long-time art editor at the magazine, Françoise Mouly. "My research is to go around looking for a particular subject until a much funnier one hits me in the head."

When I visited that afternoon, six months after this interview was published, McCall was no longer able to leave his apartment. During our initial email exchange, he'd written that he had Parkinson's disease, a progressive neurological disorder that can affect mobility. Recently, it had become more of a struggle.

"After three ho-hum years it went on a rampage," he wrote. "It's screwed me up."

The catastrophes were gradual at first: a decline in agility, a problem with his grasp, which wasn't stiffness, exactly, but a wiring issue. The signal between his brain and his hand was being intercepted, making it impossible to hold an object. Then, as if the earth had tilted, his balance went.

"I can't travel alone, not even a block, for fear of falling and busting a hip, which means the nursing home," he'd written.

The light in McCall's apartment was sharp, an artist's light, illuminating and shadowless. After he greeted me at the door, we sat together in the whiteness of his living room. Me on a white couch, him on a white armchair, his back to the bank of windows along the east wall that faced Central Park. The windows were open, and after the initial disquieting silence I could hear the rotors of a helicopter spinning above us and the rush and honk of traffic along Park Avenue below. There was also the sound of McCall's lighter, snapping, sparking, and failing to light his cigar, two, three times before it caught and he puffed, once, twice, and a quiver of smoke rose and settled above our heads. The smell, pungent and sweet, would linger in my clothes and hair long after I left. His caregiver, placid, strong, and quietly firm, hovered on the margins of our conversation.

McCall was eighty-four, the same age as my father. He had a stubbly white beard and a thick head of short, spiked white hair. His eyes, sunken and hound-dog-like, were a vibrant blue. He's a humorist, a writer, a memoirist, and he is an artist, although he doesn't call himself that. The term conjures stuffy scholars, Old Masters, Rembrandt, Goya, Picasso. It smacks of snobbery, and of taking oneself too seriously. For a satirist, this would be a problem. McCall is self-taught and cut his teeth illustrating for automotive advertising. His early career remains etched into his present work — shiny cars slink through the frames and zany ads appear on background billboards, adding a secondary dimension to the central action of his satirical paintings, which often grace the cover of *The New Yorker*. He's written and illustrated ten books, sometimes collaborating with other creative people. Most recently, he worked with David Letterman on *This Land Was Made for You and Me (But Mostly Me): Billionaires in the Wild*, published in 2013, a satirical book about the rich. He's a prolific humour writer, churning out short, farcical pieces on subjects like what Trumpcare might look like, or the act of online shopping in North Korea. His 1997 memoir, *Thin Ice: Coming of Age in Canada*, details his unhappy childhood spent pinned under his alcoholic parents. The work is laced with humour but filled with sorrow and crippling self-doubt. It's also the story of his escape. Physically, he left Simcoe, Ontario, and then Toronto for New York, but mentally, he had retreated into writing and art long before. "I'm not a humorist by nature, but I made myself sane by satirizing life, and it worked," he told me, as explanation. He sounded almost surprised.

McCall's visual art is a bizarre hybrid of prophecy and smirk, so singular and strange that he's invented his own descriptor for it: "retro-futurism." He illustrates the way people in the past envisioned the future: figures reminiscent of Dick and Jane ride in flying Model T Fords; World War Two–era helicopters construct a skyway that stretches across some vast space-age metropolis. Humorous in their outlandish optimism, they are also like a riddle: What is a futuristic nostalgia for an imagined time that never came to pass?

And yet many of his illustrative works are rooted in the present, confounding the ageist notion that older artists are only able to engage with the past. A 2016 cover for the *The New Yorker*, "Glass Houses," addresses the spate of steel-and-glass towers that are plaguing the New York City skyline, housing people who live with no curtains. This affords them an unblemished view of the city but, instead of looking out, they watch screens, gigantic and miniature. They are mirrors to their neighbours—other people encased in glass, star-ing into rectangular voids, but never looking at the views out their endless windows.

They are trapped inside, by choice.

McCall spoke rapidly; his voice, affected by Parkinson's, had grown raspy and quiet, and there were moments of silence as he gathered his breath. He was difficult to understand, another facet of the disease: a thickness of speech, a blurring of words. I sometimes repeated myself when I misunderstood his answers. For this reason, I asked twice about his art practice, and each time he told me he couldn't paint, or that he couldn't hold a brush. Even when I listened carefully and made out what he was telling me, it was as if I wasn't able to comprehend the concept, or its implica-tions. I'd seen his illustrations in the most recent issue of the *The New Yorker*, which prompted me to ask if he used an assistant.

"No assistant," he said. "I just don't paint anymore."

I remembered, then, working for magazines in my early twenties and watching the editors lay out Christmas features in the sweat of a July heatwave. To work in magazine publishing requires a certain level of clairvoyance. Everything is done weeks, sometimes months, in advance.

"Come," McCall said, sitting forward, straining as he lifted himself from the armchair. Once upright, he swayed slightly, and his caregiver caught his arm with surprising strength for her small frame. I followed them down the hall and into McCall's studio.

"My life," he said. Images of friends and family were pinned to the wall facing us, and miniature classic cars lined a small shelf below. On the opposite side of the room there was a tall cabinet of long, thin drawers where he kept his sketches (organized into categories including *New Yorker* Covers, Unpublished Works, Published Art, Archive, and Other). An old sink sat just below the cabinet, tipped on its side. McCall's caregiver fished a folding chair out of a pile in the corner and opened it, instructing him to sit. He waved her off, swayed some, then acquiesced and sat down amidst the chaotic hum of his studio space.

Along the north wall, a small, unfinished painting sat propped on a large architect's easel. In the foreground of the painting was a jogger, wearing a red tank top and running shorts, heading straight towards the viewer along a path that wound through Central Park, or perhaps a green space in one of the boroughs—this was, after all, intended to be a *New Yorker* cover. In the work's arrested state, the runner had no feet: his left leg, lifted high at the knee, disappeared into the blank space of the page somewhere around the ankle; his right leg was lost at mid-calf. There were no people seated on the benches that lined the runner's trail. The background, the green space of the park, the trees, the pigeons—those sly, grey birds that occupy the corners of so many of McCall's illustrations—were missing. There was no New York skyline. There was no sky.

The painting of the runner looked as if the artist had paused midway through, paint still wet, to step out for lunch or to answer a phone call, and that he would return shortly. And yet, the space around the easel was nearly impassable, jammed with the detritus of a life's work. The sink suggested this room had become a holding tank for defunct objects on their way out of the apartment. Useless, replaced, it lay there waiting for someone strong enough to carry it out and dispose of it, however one does such a thing in the heart of Manhattan. The studio had the feel of a house abandoned in an emergency. This was not an organized move: there were no carefully wrapped objects or labelled boxes. The occupant of this space had never intended to leave.

"Two years ago, I did sketches, and then I drew it," McCall said, gesturing to the painting of the runner. "I tried to do it three times, and every time it was worse."

He stood, then, and moved closer to the easel, his caretaker shadowing his movements.

"I'll show you," he said.

He gripped a pencil, lifted his hand to the page, and tried to follow the contours of the runner's left leg, to sketch out the runner's left foot. He was unable to harness his movements. He threw down the pencil, having demonstrated to me the realities and frustrations of being an artist unable to create.

"It was awful and I had to quit."

He had called Mouly and told her that he couldn't finish.

"It broke her heart," he said. "Broke mine, too."

"What would it look like if it were finished?" I asked.

"The old people are running and the kids are all sitting around on the benches," he said.

As with his other works, this one told a story both of the city and of a greater cultural moment. The runners in Central Park are getting older, elderly even, in a kind of slow-morphing geriatric marathon, and, at the same time, the young are becoming increasingly sedentary. Because the painting was unfinished, I couldn't know this for certain, but I suspected the young people sitting on the benches would be slumped and inert and, as with the people in the glass towers, gazing into their smartphones, oblivious of what was happening around them, distracted by the infinite pathways of their tiny machines. They wouldn't be noticing their elders, sailing by — fit, for now. They wouldn't see them, their worth, and how hard they were working to survive, to thrive. *Look up*, I wanted to shout at the ghost figures who weren't there. Look up and see what you're missing, before they're all gone.

McCALL SHIFTED AWAY FROM the painting of the runner and I followed him into the adjacent room, where an open laptop was flanked by towers of books and papers on a mahogany desk. This was his office, which doubled as the dining room. One end of the dining table was also covered with piles of papers and books. The desk was pushed up against an open window, from which you could see the windows of the apartment building opposite and a sliver of Central Park. There was an office chair—black, ergonomic—at the desk, and this was where McCall spent his days, at work on his second memoir. He wrote for ten hours a day, and had kept up this pace for six months. He wrote one version, then deleted it, then rebuilt the structure, and rearranged the parts. He would write a chapter over a series of days, then reread it and revise it, and write some more. He was writing in a fever, and it was, he said, all he did.

"It's frustrating, but it's good, and it's deeply meaningful to me. I only had the idea last February of how to do it right," he said. "I think it's a good idea."

I heard an echo of my father in those words. On the morning last summer, when I'd discovered him unpinning pen-and-ink drawings from his corkboard. *I had an idea this morning over breakfast,* he'd said. *I think it will work.*

McCall said that if he couldn't write, he wouldn't have anything else to do. He wasn't able to wander the city, and he couldn't draw or paint, but he could still escape, as he'd done during his difficult childhood. While writing, he could follow whatever path he chose, uncover surprises and secrets and stories previously unexplored, and some might eventually fit into the structure of his book while the rest might remain part of his exploration, but nevertheless, every day, he went somewhere else and discovered something new, even though he never left his apartment.

"If I couldn't write anymore, I'd probably kill myself," he said, then paused, and took a breath. "This book will probably be the last thing that I do."

I didn't stay long with McCall, mostly because I was concerned about my father and unable to suppress the looping film reel (the doorknob, the elevator, the revolving door). As we said goodbye, I told him that I was looking forward to reading his memoir. He nodded and said, "If I finish."

I didn't detect a tone of defeat in this comment. It was the regular kind of thing that artists say, every day, as they work at a project that they think could be great, with some finesse, with the right direction, structure, and content, but that they know isn't quite finished yet. They know that there is still work to do.

IT WAS NEARLY FOUR by the time I returned to the hotel, and my father had been alone for three hours. I held my breath as the elevator jostled its way up to our floor, and again as I put the key in the lock. I opened the door to see my father sitting at the roll-top bureau, surrounded by his felt-tipped markers, his inkwell, and his fountain pens. He'd made three 4-by-5-inch drawings in my absence, all inspired by *The Shipwreck of Don Juan*, which we'd seen the day before at the Metropolitan Museum of Art's retrospective show of work by the nineteenth-century French artist Eugène Delacroix. We'd sat in front of the painting for some time, resting and looking at the work. In it, a wretched tangle of human bodies overburdens the boat, the port gunwale lunging low into the waves, the line between life and death close. They are afloat, but barely. They must sacrifice one to save the many—and if you look closely, you can see they are drawing lots. They will not throw the loser overboard, but, instead, they will consume them. The water roils beneath the boat. Above, the sky is on the verge of twilight, hinting at darkness to come. Delacroix had been influenced by Géricault's *Raft of the Medusa*, which he'd seen in its early stages, having posed for his artist friend—Delacroix is the corpse lying face-down in the centre foreground, his hand outstretched. He'd been so inspired by the work that he'd run home to his own studio, alight with the possibilities of paint. Géricault influenced Delacroix, who, in turn, inspired a century's worth of artists to paint, and to see, in a new way, one that critics would term "impressionism" for its instantaneous feel—a reaction to, rather than a reproduction of, nature. As we'd sat there at the Met, my father had pointed to the painting's sky, saying he could see hints of Monet's *Water Lilies* in Delacroix's heavens. Monet had just begun painting the series the year that *The Shipwreck of Don Juan* was completed. "You can find all of us...in Delacroix," Cézanne said, and my father echoed.

The first two of my father's drawings, inspired by Delacroix's vessel itself, were sharply sketched, featuring the stern of an empty boat, running diagonally across the page. Only the third hinted at the chaos in Delacroix's painting. A whorl of small figures inside an ear-shaped mass; an ominous green puddling in the hull; and a curious turquoise splash just beyond the action.

My father had conjured the painting from memory because he had forgotten that he'd bought a postcard of *The Shipwreck of Don Juan* in the gift shop we'd wandered through while exiting the show. He had a knowledge of art encyclopedic enough that he could pull up any image he wished, an internal art-history slide library, and yet, he could not rely on his memory from the day before, when he'd carefully studied the rack of postcards until he found the one he was looking for—the boat—selected it, paid for it, then tucked it into the pocket of his suit coat. Seeing the painting had stirred his imagination, and he'd carried this inspiration through that day, overnight, and into the next afternoon when he'd started to draw. It didn't matter that he'd forgotten the act of buying the postcard. That was ultimately inconsequential; the memory was lost but the idea, the spark, remained with him.

I picked up the small paper bag from the museum which had been lying on the coffee table in our room, found the postcard, and handed it to my father.

"Oh, Em, you got one for me, thank you," he said, beaming, taking the image and propping it up so that he could look at it and continue drawing.

BEFORE MEETING MCCALL, SOMETIME during our initial email exchanges, I'd sent him an article about a possible link between Parkinson's and creativity. A study mentioned in the piece suggests that the disease opens new pathways in the brain, enabling creative thought and expression in people who'd previously left these regions unexplored. The artist interviewed for the story was bespectacled, wore her hair in an unassuming bob, and described her day job as "boring."

Her work, which was showcased throughout the article, was dreamlike, hinting at the figurative — maybe it's a horse's head, maybe it's a landmass — and the colours vibrated like live wires. Some paintings were dark — ominous, heavy brushstrokes portended a storm brewing, some looming disaster — but, nearly always, there was a swath of riotous colour which she described, optimistically, as "hope."

Despite her suggestion that she'd never been artistic, her words were poetic. "My life is like a bowl that was turned upside down," she said, conjuring a Hebrew expression to illustrate her uncanny neurological shift. The story was uplifting, mysterious, and strange, but reading it a second time, after visiting McCall and witnessing his struggle, I saw that this was a fairy tale. It's not that I doubted the science, or even the woman's talent as an artist. Her work did what only the very best art could — it was surprising, and it showed us something new. This woman, I felt, had been freed from a tower prison, had let down her hair. Her release was a kind of magic. Scrolling through the images of her work, I thought of McCall's unfinished painting. Then I went back to the beginning of the article and, maybe for the first time, noticed the headline: "The Most Dangerous Muse: Parkinson's Disease Gave Her the Gift of Creativity." Now, the headline seemed offhanded to me, a little glib.

Life mutates in old age. Your state of being in one phase can be unrecognizable in the next. Say your muse is the city—its streets, the human interactions and the multitudes of cars, its soaring towers, but also the crevices and corners, the ubiquitous pigeons... and then, one day, you're barred from entering, left outside the gates. Before the day I left my father alone to visit with McCall, I'd underestimated aging, that powerful inevitable force.

"Old age is a massacre," wrote Philip Roth in his novel *Everyman*. And yet, in devastation there is always new life, a birth. Berries grow best in the charred remains of the forest fire. The winter storm uncovers a lost sand beach. There is the lilac bush whose snapped branch has bloomed unseasonably after the hurricane in Katha Pollitt's poem "Lilacs in September." In the final stanza the poet asks, *What will unleash / itself in you / when your storm comes?*

Maybe you will become an elderly long-distance runner who trains in Central Park. Maybe the rewiring of your brain will stir something ferocious inside of you, and the manifestations will be electric paintings that cause viewers to gasp and hold their breath. Death might be a musician's feverish inspiration, his four last compositions his most intense and beautiful, a bloom of a finale.

"I've grown more observant with age," McCall told me during the afternoon we spent together. "I still have ideas."

In his studio, the runner, his leg lifted, his feet absent, remains on the easel, untouched; the sink lies on its side waiting for a journey elsewhere, and the pinned photographs curl at the edges. McCall is in the next room, his back turned on this space, seated at a table pushed up against an open window, writing, writing, writing.

ON OUR FINAL MORNING I sat with my father in the bar of a tiny restaurant in LaGuardia Airport. Above a line of liquor bottles, I could see planes taxiing along the runway. There was no Delacroix here. No *Starry Night*. Passengers embarking on a journey home, or somewhere far away, new or familiar, were squished like sardines into the too-narrow space of the bar. My shoulder touched the woman next to me, we were so close. She leaned over and quietly told me that she was very drunk and wondered if she sounded okay to travel.

"Am I slurring?" she asked, then erupted into loud, unnerving laughter. My father caught my eye and raised his brows, questioning me. I'd tell him about the woman's comment later. He'd find it amusing. The menu was long and complicated. I vetted the choices, trying to simplify for my dad. He decided on the minestrone—the elusive soup that he'd been ordering at all the restaurants we'd visited, though it had been on none of the menus. Nor did it feature today.

I coaxed him toward a different soup, a chowder.

"Yes, a chowder," he said. "That would be nice."

As we waited for our meals to arrive, the talk turned to memory. Specifically, its loss. It was the first time we'd talked frankly about dementia, although we didn't pronounce its name. I'd been recounting some of my visit with Bruce McCall the previous day, how he'd struggled to use his pencil, and how because of this his final *New Yorker* cover would remain unfinished. But, I'd added, he'd been working on his memoir, and with his mind unaffected and his fingers able to type, he planned to finish. I hoped I sounded optimistic.

"I'm—" my dad began, then halted. "Well, you know what I am."

"Does it affect your drawing?"

"No," he said, "it doesn't. Not when I put pen to page."

For now, his secret prayer had been answered.

WHO WAS THE TRIP to New York City for? The anonymous commenter on the internet travel site had asked this question and I'd heard him, her, them, whoever they were, asking me this question as I pushed through the crowds of people at the Museum of Modern Art who did not care how old or frail my father was. Who was this trip for? I asked myself, as we inched across the city in taxis and my father asked, often, which way we were going, which destination (almost always an art gallery; once, a Broadway show). Was it for him? I asked myself as my father, tired by the third morning, opted to stay in the hotel room for a few hours. At times over the past few days, I'd felt this trip was for my dad. This was most likely our final voyage—the last days we'd ever spend together in a foreign city, as we had when we were both younger and in very different periods of our lives. It was the last time we'd wander the hallowed halls of the Met, or MoMA, or see a Broadway show, maybe the last time we'd linger over hotel banquet-style breakfasts with white tablecloths on the tables and silver-domed rolltop chafers open to reveal bacon, eggs, waffles, French toast, and whatever else you desired. Who was this trip for? In the end, it was for my dad, but it was also for me. It was for both of us, together.

Cross-Stitch

THE NIGHT AFTER VISITING Bruce McCall in New York City, I dreamt that I was in his apartment when his caregiver began readying herself to leave for home. She was fetching her purse, putting on her jacket and shoes, and she gave a little wave to say goodbye as she stood, perched in the threshold of the doorway, and then she closed the door and was gone. I was still there, or at least, I was witnessing the scene as some kind of omniscient observer. This can't possibly be how this works, I thought. Surely Bruce will need assistance to prepare his evening meal, possibly even to eat it, and while getting ready for bed.

I woke just after five a.m., slowly blinking into the darkness of my hotel room, feeling panicked. The dream had felt real enough that I forced myself to go over the final moments of my visit to Bruce's apartment the day before. He'd given me two of his books, and I'd asked him to sign them. He tried, but was unable. I re-envisioned the scene, and in it, his caregiver was standing with him, holding his arm. I was certain, then, of her presence — because I remembered feeling ashamed at how I could have spent the afternoon speaking with Bruce, witnessing his inability to paint, and still asked him to sign a book, as if the acts of handwriting and painting were so distinct that losing one didn't necessarily mean losing the other. I remembered feeling particularly embarrassed at having a witness to this transaction. Also, I'd met Bruce's wife that afternoon. She lived with him. He would never truly be alone. Still, I backtracked again and replayed the final few seconds, as we'd stood in the front hall. I could see the caretaker standing at Bruce's side, and I could remember how she'd waved goodbye to me, in the same way she'd waved in my dream, an uncomplicated, friendly parting, before the door shut and I was briefly alone in the small foyer waiting for the elevator.

I don't think you need to be a Jungian analyst to interpret this dream, to make the leap that this dream was not about Bruce. It was about my dad, about the terrible panic of leaving him alone in the hotel room, but also the larger, overarching anxiety that had been crackling on the horizon like a distant forest fire. I could smell the smoke, see the haze in the air, but wasn't yet affected by the impending ravages as it burned forward. The question was, with my mother also growing older, who would look after my dad as this disease progressed?

I VISITED A CARE home in Stratford, a request from my mother, during the winter after my father was diagnosed with dementia. This seemed a far-off possibility, an unlikely scenario, we both felt, but we also agreed that it would be prudent, nonetheless, to look into it. The facility was slightly removed from the lights of the theatre, the red-brick charm of the main commercial thoroughfare and its throng of tourists, the restaurants and trinket shops. Instead, it was located in a postwar suburb on the edge of town. There were cornfields in the distance. It was a timber-frame building, a construction not unlike my father's studio in Wellesley, also built by Mennonite carpenters — warm wood, light-filled, practical and sturdy. After arriving, I turned off my car's engine and heard the faint wail of a country song coming from the white sedan parked next to me. A tousle-haired woman sat smoking in the driver's seat, staring listlessly over the wheel, the windows rolled up so that she was encased in swirls of smoke. We locked eyes, briefly, then she looked away and I got out of my car and walked towards the centre.

"Here is an example of one of our retirement rooms," my guide, Joanne, told me, as she showed me inside what looked like a hotel room with an en suite and separate living area. There were generic paintings on the wall, benign floral arrangements that I thought looked as if they were purchased from a box furniture store. Perhaps they had been in place when the resident arrived. I suspected that there were policies regarding the hanging of works of art, and wondered if my father would be permitted to cover one of the walls in cork and pin his drawings there. I'd recently read about a care home designed specifically for people with dementia in Langley, B.C. The facade of the linked homes was typical of the region, colourful clapboard and peaked roofs, but the interior was only one storey for ease of wheelchair access. Inside, works of art were used as way-finders, but the content was restricted to landscapes and still lifes. "Avoid potentially confusing abstracts, such as Rothkos and Mondrians," suggested the architect of these dementia spaces. The comment seemed ridiculous and old-fashioned. That would surely never apply to my father, I thought.

Joanne told me that a single woman lived in the room we were touring. Her bed was small and tightly made, her shelves lined with framed family photographs. In one, an older, white-haired man looked as if he'd been surprised by the photographer, his mouth open, his eyebrows raised high.

"You bring everything but the curtains because they need to be fire-retardant," Joanne said. "I've always found that rule strange, how everything else can go up in flames, but the curtains have to be fireproof."

I briefly imagined the home on fire. It seemed an odd thing to say. But maybe it was part of her repertoire, and she said it to every visitor. She'd already finished her first tour of the day when I'd arrived at nine a.m.

I'd worried that visiting the care home would be emotional, but instead I felt nothing. This place was an example scenario, one that felt distant, and for a future father who did not resemble the one I knew today.

"The wait list can take between six months and a year," Joanne said, as we walked along the stretch of corridors, across the industrial carpet the colour of dishwater flanked by beige walls, and towards the exit. Six months didn't seem long to me at all, not in a facility with so few units, all of them occupied. I was flummoxed by this arithmetic until I realized: the tenants who lived there always moved on. It was a transience that came with dementia's creep or other difficult age-related illnesses, ones that required more than a friendly helping hand, eventually making this semi-independent set-up impossible — and leaving, inevitable. Also, probably, a number of residents died there.

On the drive home, I passed through the small towns of my youth, the farmers' fields stretching out to the horizon on both sides of the highway. On the final portion of my journey, I turned off the highway and travelled the backroads that I'd driven every morning and every afternoon with my father during elementary school, retracing our long-ago drives in a landscape that was both familiar and, in places, unrecognizably changed by housing developments and shopping malls. Looking out at the world that had inspired so many of my father's middle-career works, I tried to remember the view from the window of the room that Joanne had showed me, or at least to imagine what lay beyond the sill. It might have faced south, towards the distant cornfields, but more likely the view was of the drab suburb with its chock-a-block homes arranged in a tidy semicircle around the cul-de-sac. There were several questions that I'd planned to ask during my tour, but found I could not—the words arrested on my tongue, the notions suddenly frivolous, outrageous, even. Do you serve wine with dinner? What about transportation to the park during the summer music series, could that be arranged? Could someone take my father golfing? Can you see any trees from the windows of the residences? Would there be anything to draw? For example, graveyards with older, decaying tombstones? Anything like that nearby?

I couldn't imagine telling Joanne, who had a kind, earnest face, that my father liked to sketch in cemeteries. Besides, I'd known instinctively, as soon as I'd arrived at the home, that if my father could drink wine, wander graveyards while sketching *en plein air*, golf and attend summer concerts, he wasn't going to be living there. The main question I wanted to ask concerned the most important facet of my father's later life: How would you help him to keep making art? How would you feed his creativity, even when diminished and faint? What lengths would you travel to reach his imagination as he neared the end?

MONTHS LATER, I VISITED a facility with an entirely different approach to aging than the first home I'd toured. Based in Toronto and called the Performing Arts Lodge, to qualify you must have worked in the entertainment industry for fifteen years, which meant the tenants were

actors and television personalities but also people who'd
worked in electrical, lighting, and stage direction. It was
affordable housing with a long wait list, and residents
were largely older, but it was also a haven for younger
performers whose lives were equally precarious, those
living with illness or disability, in poverty, or, through
the nature of spotty contract work, isolated from their
peers in the industry. It wasn't a care home, but there
were on-site health services and various supports for
residents, including a food bank and counselling services. There was a decent-sized library stacked with
Canadian literature — Alice Munro's *The Love of a Good
Woman*, Lawrence Hill's *The Illegal* — and the complete
works of Shakespeare, and there was a gym, a dance
studio, and a full-sized stage in the dining room. There
was also an on-site jazz lounge called the Celebrity Club,
which was where I spent the bulk of my visit to PAL.

Being in the club was dreamlike, not in an ethereal
or fuzzy or even particularly beautiful sense, because
the space looked like any small jazz lounge might, with
its mahogany bar, dark wood panelling and burgundy
colour scheme. No, it was dreamlike in the way the
bizarre becomes accepted as fact, and in the way that
celebrities are characters in your dreams and can cas-
ually wend their way into your life's narrative, which
is what happened when I ordered a glass of Merlot at
the bar and realized that the bartender was Dini Petty,
a broadcaster and talk-show host I remembered from
my childhood and teen years. She looked unchanged,
as if she hadn't aged, which made me wonder if I was

misremembering the dates. (I wasn't.) Also, there's a notion of what a typical older woman looks like, or even how she behaves, that they are sweet grannies with short grey curls who wear cardigans and beige walking shoes and call everyone in their vicinity "dear." Petty was none of these things and, clearly, she never would be. Neither was Lillian Grudeff, an elderly jazz singer, lipstick-mouthed and frail, wearing a velour dress and thigh-high boots, a black beret tilted over her fire-engine-red hair. She'd arrived early, wheeled her walker up to her table, and lowered herself carefully into place, waiting for the show to begin. The opening act was a jazz pianist named Peter Hill, and when he started playing, Grudeff slowly, with steely determination, lifted herself from the table, held her walker tight, and began to sway.

Most Friday nights, she approached the booker with a message: "I've got a sore throat tonight, sweetheart, but I'll do a number for you when it clears up." The jazz singer's throat had been sore for twenty years. It was a fantasy, and yet, watching her fluid, harmonic sway, it felt possible that she could step up to the microphone at any moment. It was this possibility that mattered.

A younger man, thin, brown hair without a wisp of grey, took the jazz singer in his arms, delicately, and they swayed together. There was a sliding age scale there — people landing somewhere between fifty and a hundred — which is one of the most unusual and successful components of this residence. Those younger performers' finances and personal lives might be just as precarious, but their youth and age-related ability — standing on a stepladder to screw in a neighbour's light bulb, for example — make them a boon to the community.

The jazz singer tired and the younger man gently placed her back in her chair, then scanned the tables for a new partner. Although I'd assiduously avoided making eye contact with him, I sensed that he was moving my way.

"Please dance with me," he said. He was serious and unsmiling.

"Oh, I can't," I said. "I'm only here as an observer."

This held no sway. He took my hand and, unless I tore myself from him, causing a scene, I was going to have to dance. Up close, I saw that his youth was only surface-level, deceptive in the light and exaggerated amidst the elderly crowd. He was surely in the vicinity of fifty, although still young in this context. We wove in and around the tables as the main act, singer Marla Lukofsky, crooned "It Had to be You," and I thought, *My god, I'm so tired! Why am I dancing?* I hadn't danced with anyone, not even my husband, in years. I was tipsy from the generous glass of Merlot poured by the famous talk-show host who had surely aged, and yet appeared not to have aged at all. Was it the light? Or was it something else, more mystical and difficult to understand? This place was Never Never Land, but for elderhood, that increasingly long stretch between the traditional age of retirement and death — the space of the long afternoon followed by twilight, the magic hour.

The lounge felt like a stage set, lit for the mood, a hint of nostalgia for times gone. Black-and-white photographs lined the walls where ghosts of residents past mingled with current tenants, their head shots signed, framed, and displayed. I saw actor Eleanor Beecroft and greeted her silently as I danced by, remembering how I'd interviewed her for a student journalism project I'd done on PAL sixteen years before. Back then, she'd been the oldest resident — she'd had ninety in the crosshairs. I did some silent math as I twirled around the room with the man whose name I never learned. Eleanor would be 112 if she were still alive. I wouldn't see her tonight — at least, not in person. So long, Eleanor! There, along the far wall, was opera singer Maureen Forrester, also gone, and a photograph of the filmmaker Norman Hart, posing with Muhammad Ali. Hart, however, happened to also be there in person, sitting at a table opposite his image, watching the show. Actor Ardon Bess, who was the first Black actor to graduate from Montreal's National Theatre School, in 1968, was sitting at a high-top near the back of the room.

As we moved toward the front, we passed Elva Mai Hoover, who'd been tasked with showing me around earlier in the day, and with whom I'd eaten dinner at the club that evening. I locked eyes with her and smiled, still feeling foolish to be dancing. Hoover wore her greying hair swept back from her face, and her eyebrows were arched as if in a permanent state of intrigue, her eyes expressive and warm. Shortly after meeting her, as we'd stood side by side in the elevator, I had mentioned that I'd visited a more traditional retirement home recently. Before I'd finished my sentence, she'd eyed me, coolly.

"This is not a retirement home," she said. "Most of us are still working."

That week she'd been doing some sound dubbing for a Hallmark Christmas movie she'd filmed a month earlier, and the day before, she'd been down to the wire on an audition for a McDonald's commercial, although she didn't get the part.

My second gaffe happened as we'd toured the second-floor facilities. That afternoon, I planned to see a showcase of new plays by students in a theatre program for older adults run by Ryerson University.

"Would anyone here be involved with that program?"

I'd meant in a teaching capacity, but I hadn't been clear.

"You know they're not professionals," Elva said.

She seemed concerned that I would equate the work of amateurs with that of the residents of PAL. In the moment, I'd felt her reaction seemed a little harsh, pooh-poohing the work of the hobbyists when measured against the real thing. But when we reunited for dinner at the Celebrity Club, Elva inquired, with genuine interest, how the plays had gone. The program had run long, I admitted, but I'd enjoyed seeing the final production of a play by a woman named Pat Cochrane, whom I'd met months before when I'd sat in on the auditions for the theatre series. I'd seen sections of her play, *Here's to Catharine!*, that day, and it had stood out to me. We spoke after the auditions were over, and then again, the following week, over the phone. Pat told me that through the theatre program, she'd discovered a propensity for playwriting in her retirement years. She hadn't written plays before this new period in her life. She'd worked on but not finished a few short stories, and, once, a movie script, but had always gotten side-tracked, focused as she was on her professional career as a registered nurse working at a private school for boys in Toronto.

She'd joined the theatre program because her life had been enveloped by tragedy. Her son, who had schizo-phrenia, had died by suicide. It had defined her, in her retirement. Tragedy had become who she was. She saw an advertisement for the Ryerson program, she couldn't remember where, but something in it had piqued her interest, if only vaguely. It was a stretch, she thought, but, who knew, maybe she'd be a good actor?

"I was a terrible actor," Pat told me. "I'm very stilted on stage."

But she was good at writing plays. She had an ear for dialogue, picked up during her ten years facilitating sup-port groups for young people struggling with addiction. The work had made her aware of the rhythms of speech. She'd had to manage the conversation. No single person could dominate or weigh down the discussion, and no one could remain entirely silent, either. There needed to be balance, a narrative flow. She said that the plays arrived to her fully formed.

"I can't explain it. Very often it's when I'm sleeping.

I'll wake up with it. But often it will come to me when my mind's quite blank," she said, and I thought of Paul McCartney waking up with the tune to "Yesterday" playing in his head, and of my father's resident fairy, working on his drawings as he slept.

Her plays immediately began to win awards within the program, but, when we last spoke, she had no ambitions for a professional career. It was enough for her. It had changed how she saw herself, and how others saw her.

"Now, I define myself by what's going on in the theatre, and also my friends define me that way too. They see me as the kind of person who is resilient and has recovered rather than seeing me as a victim," Pat said. "It gives you a whole different view of yourself."

All lives are rife with struggle. For performers, work is precarious, and there are no guarantees that the audition you're preparing for this afternoon will lead to a job tomorrow—after all, Elva didn't get the role in the McDonald's commercial. By forty, Elva pointed out, jobs for women become scarce, and while there is some pension assurance, most performers have dipped into this before reaching the traditional retirement years. It means remaining on the cusp of what outsiders to the industry (your family, your friends) see as "making it." It is the terror of being sick and unable to work, with no compensation on the horizon, suddenly unable to buy groceries or pay your bills.

Residents who turn up at PAL's on-site food bank are often between the ages of fifty and sixty.

"Those can be hard times for performers because they're not yet ready to get any pensions but the industry is retiring them. The work opportunities aren't the same."

The food bank, the need for affordable housing and for a network to counter the isolation of contract theatre work—these are the reasons that PAL exists, but they also mark the difference between hobbyists and professionals. Elva felt that it was important to understand this distinction. She wasn't suggesting that there was less worth in the pursuits of volunteer or community theatre; she was underlining the precariousness of a life in the theatre versus a life of full-time work with health benefits and a pension. What was the same for Elva and Pat were the ways in which performance informed identity. Creative work, both amateur and professional, was sustaining both women in their third acts.

I LEFT THE CELEBRITY CLUB when the musicians were still playing, well into the second set, or maybe it was the last. The night felt crisp and harshly cold after the warmth of the lounge. Faintly, I could hear the piano, the singer's high notes fading as I walked west toward my hotel and the party carried forward, the young-ish man now dancing with some other woman, the celebrity bartender calling last call.

I telephoned my dad the next morning and told him about the night at PAL, about the frail and beautiful jazz singer with the sore throat, and the man who danced with all of the women in the room, including me, and he laughed, interested in the anecdotes as much as the wirings of the place. He'd been on the PAL board during his post-retirement years in Stratford, when that city had toyed with founding a local facility. He'd believed in the concept, knowing then, just as he knew now, that as a visual artist he would never be a candidate. I hadn't told him about the care home I'd visited in Stratford. This was a discussion for him to have with my mother, a private talk. To my mother, I'd reported that it was clean, beautifully crafted, and that nothing about the building had felt inherently sad, nor was it in any way dingy, but that there was no art.

This wasn't entirely true, however. I'd spent some time in the room that Joanne had shown me, with its fire-retardant curtains and the personal framed photographs. She'd encouraged me to look around, and, while walking along the back wall, I'd found myself eye-level with one of the framed floral still lifes on the wall. Initially, because of their uniformity, I'd assumed they were standard room decor, like the generic, inoffensive landscapes in motel rooms. At a closer look, I realized they were not painted, but cross-stitched. Each one was made from hundreds of tiny acts of colour choice, a craft of endless patience, something you work on bit by bit, the image taking shape only near the end. These were the tenant's work, and in their own way, remarkable, her thread-work so fine it appeared painterly. These framed works were her only clear decor choice beyond the family photos. They were symbolic of who she was—her perseverance, her ability, her creativity. I'd assumed the artworks had come with the room, but, of course, she'd brought them with her, and maybe she'd even created a few while living in that space. These were her self-artifacts, her art. These were her way-finders.

The Wreck of Hope

THE MIST CREPT IN while I was halfway up the mountain pass that snaked behind our rental home. I'd turned, out of breath, and watched as fog obscured the distant snow-covered peaks of the next peninsula, followed by the ocean, the harbour, then the little town of Ventry, where my two children were presently at school while we lived in Ireland for two months in the winter of 2019. Finally, the road to our house vanished. These soupy vistas weren't unusual for an Irish winter, particularly on the finger of land where we'd set up our temporary home on the most westerly point of Europe. I wasn't worried. I knew that if I followed the gravel path at my feet, it would guide me home.

As I neared the front door, a vague outline of a doorframe in the mist, my phone rang in my pocket. It was my mother. It would be five a.m. in Canada. I answered quickly.

"Your father is in the intensive care unit."

"Did he stay the night?"

"I'm not sure you heard me," she said, gently. "He's in the ICU, so, no, he did not come home last night."

I let myself inside, listening to my mother talk, staying silent on my end of the phone and staring out the kitchen window. The fog had settled in, would remain for some time. I could faintly make out the ancient stone wall that encircled our yard, but nothing beyond that. Could a plane take off in this dense air, I wondered?

"Do I need to come home?"

"No, I'd tell you if you needed to come home."

My father's admittance to the ICU was the culmination of a series of events that had begun several days before, during a dementia assessment by a team of specialists at a different hospital about an hour's drive from where my parents lived. A slew of experts had met with my father, asking him questions and administering cognition tests. It had been exhausting for him. By the end of the visit they'd revoked his driver's licence, overriding the hard-won driving test he'd passed just six months before. In the afternoon, one of the doctors took his pulse during the physical examination portion of the assessment. Puzzled, he pressed a stethoscope to my father's chest. There was a beat, followed by a pause, then, another beat. At twenty-seven beats per minute, his heart was performing rhythmically, but in slow motion. He'd require a pacemaker to regulate his heartbeat, the doctor informed him, but there was a wait list, so my parents were sent home.

When they set out for home that afternoon, snow was falling heavily, the wind whirling it into white-outs so that it was difficult to know if your car was on the road or straying across a farmer's field. It continued to snow all night. In the morning, the driveway was impassable. My mother took and retook my father's pulse. It dipped lower, and plateaued, never reaching more than thirty beats per minute. The snow kept falling. She looked out at the blanketed driveway, and car. She took my father's pulse again. No change, but no improvement, either. My mom was convinced that they needed medical help. She called a neighbour who owned a snow blower. He cleared the driveway in thirty minutes and brushed the snow off their car. Within an hour, my parents were on the road again.

At the medical clinic in the closest town, a nurse took my father's pulse, looked wide-eyed at my mother, and told her to go directly to the hospital. Once there, another nurse took his pulse and immediately admitted him. He was chuffed by this brisk triage, being whisked away while younger people with broken limbs or the flu remained in the waiting room. My mother sent me a photograph of my father lying on a gurney, wearing a blue hospital gown. His arm was encased in a black band with blue, red, and green wires snaking from it, spilling over the edge of his bed, attached to a machine that was monitoring his lethargic heart. According to my mother, the monitor that was installed above him emitted a constant shrieking noise. Sometimes, if my dad moved his arm vigorously, she said, he could make it stop, but mostly, because his heartbeat never managed to achieve a non-threatening rate, this shrill alert continued for the three hours that he lay waiting for a room. In the photograph he was giving the thumbs up, presumably to show that he was fine, despite the wiring, the surroundings, and the shrieking machine that I couldn't hear.

I looked at the image on my phone, then put it face-down on the kitchen table and returned to staring out the window. The fog had lifted and I could see the sea and, faintly, Macgillycuddy's Reeks, the mountain range that lay between me and the area of County Kerry where my parents had lived, part-time, over a period of twenty years. Because of this, the Irish landscape, in altered form, threaded through those decades of my father's works. One of these paintings hangs on a wall in my kitchen at home. It's a mythical but recognizable County Kerry: there are mountainous green hills, a hint of fog; dark clouds gather in the sky and, in the background, the sea glows silver as it meets the horizon. It was a landscape he knew well, one he'd drawn so often he could reproduce it from memory. In the painting there's a heathery field in the foreground, and small, black-and-white figures, captured in photographs from the early twentieth century, are nestled amidst the shrubs. Telephone poles with no wires stand as markers of human interference on the land. As with the missing table leg in the Degas masterpiece, L'Absinthe, my father omitted the wires that would have been strung between the poles. These lines might exist in reality, but they fractured the image unnecessarily in art. I sometimes felt that the painting in my kitchen was a window, and that I was looking out at my father's version of the years he spent drawing and painting in Ireland, a view that was true to both the landscape and his imagination.

IT WAS DECIDED THAT in a few days my father would be transferred to a larger hospital to have a pacemaker inserted. Before the procedure, the surgeon visited my parents and asked my mother a question: "Do you want to have your husband resuscitated?"

"I wasn't prepared for that," she told me, later, over the phone. "I mean, what other answer is there to that question?"

She'd turned to my father, lying in the hospital bed.

"I don't think you're ready to go," she said. "I think you have more to do, don't you?"

He was tired by then, growing confused. Still, he understood.

"Yes, I do."

My mom turned to face the doctor.

"He's an artist," she told him. "He has more work to do."

THERE IS AN ANECDOTE about the writer Mavis Gallant that my mother tells, one that I nearly always think of when an older person dies and someone says, as consolation, "Well, they had a long life." After meeting my mother at a literary event, Mavis had taken an interest in my maternal grandmother, a whip-smart constant reader who'd been denied a high school education because she was a woman and was needed on her family farm at home. (Later, she would lie on her entrance exam to nursing school, gaining acceptance by fudging a graduation date. She was intelligent and keen. No one questioned her place in the class.) Mavis and my grandmother were of the same generation, so the story of the farm, the barred education, the fact that my grandmother had been a constant fan of Gallant's work, interested Mavis. They were not unlike one another, despite the differences in their lives.

My mother wrote to tell Mavis when my grandmother died, buffering the information, as we all do, in the gift of my grandmother's ninety-five years—all lived in good health, and in sharp mind—and Mavis had written back, questioning that line of reasoning. She wondered: Wouldn't my grandmother have wanted a little more time? Don't we all? Another summer, perhaps? It has struck me, in the years since, that Mavis was speaking for all of us, but also for herself: her life's purpose, her art, was clear for her until the end. As Geoffrey Chaucer observed in the opening lines to his poem "The Parliament of Fowls": *The life so short, the craft so long to learn.*

THAT WEEKEND, AFTER HAVING his pacemaker installed, my father was released from hospital. He was disoriented, unsure of what had happened and why. A delirium had crept in, muddled his thoughts. It happens to nearly all elderly patients admitted to hospital.

"He doesn't know what's inside of him," my mother told me over the phone on Saturday. Then she addressed my father. "Tony, what's inside of you?"

"Guts!" he yelled, pleased with himself.

I snickered, and later relayed this incident to my children, who howled with laughter.

"Guts!" they hollered at one another, then fell down, hysterical, rolling around on the ground. They'd known that their grandfather was in hospital, and that he'd had an operation. Having proof that my father's ridiculousness was intact was a relief for them, and for me. Also, I think my father knew precisely what was inside of him.

WE WERE SITTING AT the octagonal kitchen table that had once belonged to my maternal grandmother. My father sat to my right, my mother to my left. It was an arrangement familiar from my childhood—two parents, one child—but foreign to me in adulthood. I never visited my parents alone, at least never without my children. It had been nearly two weeks since we'd returned from Ireland, and a month since my father had his pacemaker installed. I'd arrived by train the previous afternoon. It was quiet in their home. Still. A place of recovery. My parents told me the story of their ordeal over dinner, then again at breakfast. It had been a harrowing journey on which they'd faced possible death, a feat they'd survived together. It was the kind of tale that was unpleasant and frightening but that, in retrospect, was laced with humour. My mother commented, more than once, on the good-looking emergency medics who had accompanied my father on the long ambulance ride between hospitals. My father, in his hospital-induced delirium, had believed the ambulance attendants were his graduate students from the fine arts department, playing a trick on him. He was equally suspicious of a nurse whose thankless job it was to reprimand him every time he got out of bed and began readying himself to leave, which was often. Despite his predicament, my father had voraciously eaten his hospital meals, delighted by their punctual arrival and the tidy display of servings: a quiver of Jell-O, saltines wrapped in crinkly plastic, a melamine dish neatly dividing the meat and potatoes, and a small, plastic cup of water. He'd once hailed a passing nurse and inquired after my mother's meal.

"He thought he was in a restaurant," my mother told me. "He said to her, 'My wife has been waiting for her meal a long time now.'"

"Well, she had been waiting a long time," my dad said, feigning indignance.

I laughed, feeling relieved by his humour.

"How did the nurse react?"

"She got it," my mother said. "She understood."

ON THE SECOND MORNING of my visit, my mother and I decided to take a drive down to the cottage to see the frozen lake. I was surprised when my father brightened at the idea and announced that he'd join us. I had assumed he'd been staying indoors, both to recuperate and because of the weather. That winter had been treacherous. There had been an assault of ice: great, blueish shields had enveloped yards and fields while jagged, impenetrable mountains had formed at the edges of driveways and sidewalks where snow had been cleared. It lay, too, invisible and lurking underfoot, disguised as pavement, asphalt, or dry road. It was a dangerous winter to be old.

The night before, I'd run my fingers over the bump on my father's chest where the pacemaker, barely larger than a business card, had been slipped beneath his skin to orchestrate the beat of his heart, which was now measured and constant, like the tick-tock of the metronome that had once sat atop his grand piano. A faint breeze of nausea had blown through me. I've always blanched at medical interference with the body. Needles, stitches, any form of surgery, and my stomach creeps into my throat, the lights flicker, and I go down, sometimes hard. This feeling was now compounded by the anxious knowledge that the mechanical device was keeping my father alive. Poor, weary heart, there were only so many times it could beat unassisted.

My mother's car was barge-like. She steered down the cottage lane as if she were driving an icebreaker through Arctic waters, and the frozen ground crunched and shattered under the weight of the tires. I worried about getting stuck. There was no one down there at this time of year: the scattering of wooden clapboard cottages stood still, temporarily deserted. I briefly imagined how I'd heave my weight behind the hulking car while my mother stepped on the gas, and my father, barred from the wheel and exertion, would direct. We had a history of getting our cars stuck, a vocational hazard for my parents, who routinely drove down muddy, abandoned country lanes to explore the possibilities of the unknown, forgotten pieces of the landscape where marks of the past persisted into the present—the wallpapered rooms of an abandoned farmhouse, or a germinating tombstone, the deceased's name slowly being obscured by lichen. The familiar sounds that accompanied these journeys remained fresh in my memory: spinning wheels, spattering mud, the sharp knock on the doors of deep-country strangers, my mother asking to use their telephone. The tow truck's winch; the groan of a car pulled free.

My dad had been to the lake earlier in the week, I learned, and he had been keen to get back. We walked together, shuffling across the slick white ice. I offered him my arm for balance, conscious that I, too, could slip, and bring him down with me. Some men might have found this loss of autonomy humiliating, but my father didn't seem to mind.

WHILE WAITING TO BOARD my train in Toronto the day before, I'd witnessed an older man fall. Because I had the dog with me, I was instructed to stand near the front of the line where people gathered to preboard. The business-class passengers were admitted first and they began to slowly disappear through an archway and onto the narrow escalator that led up to the train platform. I was bent forward, balancing an overly heavy duffel bag against my back—a poor luggage choice, I realized, too late—while reining in the struggling dog on his leash. I was distracted by the sound of a prolonged buzzer, an alarm. The escalator, of which I could see only a few steps, abruptly stopped, and I watched a brown paper gift-bag tumble down the final three steps, the balls of tissue paper that had cradled its contents spilling out the open top and rolling, white and crumpled, to land a few paces away from me. I thought of the shopkeeper packing the bag, carefully cushioning the object inside. Had all that tissue been put in place for just this kind of accident? Then I noticed the top of a man's balding head, the wispy white hairs askew, and I slowly understood that this meant the man had fallen backwards, and that he was now lying face-up in the middle of the escalator, his legs pointed up the stairs, his head pointed down. The gift bag he'd carried, flung by his helpless arms, had arced over his falling body, landing seconds before him. He lay there, unmoving, as a collective gasp arose from the other passengers in line—simultaneously drawn breaths, hands lifted to cover mouths. Even the dog, for a moment, stopped his desperate pull, and sat. Someone in the crowd said a hard, crisp "Fuck."

Train porters rushed to help, but it was a slow process, the area too narrow to find a place to stand on either side of the fallen man, in order to reach under his arms and pull him up to his feet. Gradually, however, the top of the head lifted, or was lifted, and then disappeared from view. Several minutes passed before a tall, white-haired man in a black sweater limped quickly from the archway and into the nearby waiting room, out of sight. He'd been up-righted, but the crowd understood that this wasn't a moment to cheer. He had been broken in some way, if not physically, then in pride. He forcibly averted his gaze from the hundreds of people that had witnessed his fall, our expressions of concern laced with the lurid need to know what had happened. A small woman of similar age followed him, half-running to keep up with his pace. He had to have been hurt, but he was determined to walk, unassisted, in the desperate urge to disappear. I could imagine what would follow: the woman's whispered phone conversations with adult children, detailing the fall, and the refusal on the man's part to acknowledge that anything had changed, when, in fact, everything would be different, in some way, going forward.

I saw the man who'd fallen once more, while on the train. My stop had been called and I was walking through the first-class cabin to get to the baggage car and retrieve the dog. The man was sitting in a single seat, his wife nearby, perhaps, although, in an attempt at subtlety, I didn't turn to check. I looked at the man briefly as I passed, took in his white hair, now smoothed into place, the slope of his shoulders, the reflection of the passing landscape blurred and moving across the lenses of his glasses. His eyes beneath, open and watchful. He'd yielded to disaster but had ultimately escaped, persevered: limping and hurt, but fiercely present, he kept moving forward.

STANDING AT THE FOOT of the beach, where in summer the grass gave way to rocks, it looked as if the waves had frozen mid-break. They were a jagged crash of grey ice dotted, strangely, with rocks and sand from the lake bottom. Some angry storm had churned up the lakebed and thrown it onto the ice surface, now a range of mountainous, unmoving waves. Beyond that, ice pans floated by in a swiftly moving current. The exposed water was grey, a reflection of the winter sky, which was pocked with steel-coloured clouds. There was a faint line of blue at the horizon. A string of geese, silhouetted in the distance, flew east. The unfrozen waves broke at the ice bank, sending spray nearly ten feet into the air, and also rushing underneath, roaring, and dragging the stones.

"Caspar David Friedrich," my dad said, referencing the nineteenth-century German Romantic artist.

The winter scene conjured Friedrich's best-known work, a desolate northern icescape, beautiful but haunting, and edged in terror. In the painting, sepia-toned shards of ice, like tectonic plates, have met and cracked upwards into jagged ice mountains. At first glance, Friedrich's painting appears wild and uninhabited, but a closer look reveals the hull of an overturned ship, its mast just visible behind a giant, tomb-like ice shard. There are no sailors scrambling atop the ice pans; the land is still, life arrested—though at what point is unclear. Was this scene painted months after the ship sank, as the ice had begun to melt, revealing winter's secret crimes? Was it painted years after the disaster, or the morning after? The painting is titled *The Sea of Ice*, but is often mislabelled as *The Wreck of Hope*. A more sombre and apt name for this painting, perhaps; or, at least, for the human tragedy depicted within. Yet, though the ship had wrecked, nature prevailed; so perhaps naming the work for the ice was a better choice after all. The painting didn't sell in Friedrich's lifetime. As with so many artists, his fame came posthumously.

I'd understood my father's shorthand, the name of a long-dead German artist uttered on the banks of a winter lake, and how he was communicating through image, through a shared history, through art.

My dad wasn't wearing a hat and the wind lifted his white hair, showing the reddening scalp underneath. I thought his coat looked thin. And yet, he was not shivering as I was. He was bewitched by the water's frothy ice peaks.

"That looks like a giant rock," he said, pointing to a large, greyish lump lying in the divot of a frozen wave.

"I think it's just an ice chunk."

"It might be our rock."

There was an underwater boulder that sat about twenty feet into the water. It had been there since I could remember. Over the summers we'd spent at the lake, my dad would walk a straight line from the corner of the cottage porch into the water and find the rock for me, lift me up onto it, toss me from it into the lake so that I would soar, for a moment, before hitting the water and submerging. He still swam in the lake. Last August, during a heatwave, he came to the beach every afternoon, his swim trunks on, a towel thrown over his shoulder. He'd move slowly across the pebbles towards the water, turn once to line himself up with the corner of the porch, and walk straight out to the big rock.

As we stood, side by side, looking at the frozen lake, I was overcome with the urge to retreat from this battered landscape, to go inside the cottage where the air would be cold but windless, providing some shelter from the relentless weather, but my father was still marvelling at the ice, so I remained in place. If he could roam as he'd done in the past, he'd maybe have returned to sketch the icy vista that had reminded him of Friedrich. But he couldn't. I understood, then, why my mother hadn't balked at having him join us, despite the ice, despite his heart. That brutal winter, the brutalities visited on him — he'd survived both. He deserved the freedom to wonder at it all.

Sun in an Empty Room

THERE WAS SOMETHING MY father wanted to show me. But first, there was lunch. We'd eaten together, sitting in a booth in the town's one restaurant, a shaft of early spring light illuminating our table. I was visiting my parents for a second time that year, staying at our cottage. I was checking on my father. After we'd finished eating, we walked across a small park to the bank, a squat red-brick square in the centre of the village, to see a number of his drawings that were stored there in ten narrow, steel cases, each one housing roughly a hundred works. These drawings spanned the arc of my father's career. They were the ones that he considered his very best.

The tellers, who were all women, knew my father by name. They welcomed him back, asked after his days, and offered to hang his coat. I suspected that this had become a habitual visit for my father, and my hunch was

confirmed when I filled out the sign-in log. His angular slanted signature appeared weekly, sometimes daily,
meaning that he'd visited his drawings often since leaving them in the care of the bank. I thought of Lee Krasner
in her final years, how she'd stopped making art but liked
to surround herself with her work, engaging with her
aesthetic, acknowledging where she'd come from, her
whole life before her in the marks of her past, because,
she said, "Even when I'm just looking, I am working."

The vault was the safest place for my father's drawings; the steel boxes could withstand weight, water,
and fire, and no doubt any bank robber would overlook these works on paper in favour of the treasures in
other vaults: the mother-of-pearl earrings, the Rolexes,
the stacks of neatly gathered cash. We edged ourselves
into a small, grey cubicle clearly meant for one, and
with some protest, my father agreed to sit in the sole
chair as we sifted through the story of his artistic life.

Here was the series of panoramic sketches he'd done
of Wellesley Pond in the eighties and nineties, the view
from the largest of his backyard studios. They were
increasingly abstract: trees became ambiguous shadows, the reflection on the water a shimmer. Above
one of these sketches was a series of tiny equations,
which he'd needed to transform this small image to the
9-by-48-inch oil-on-Masonite that it would become in
Wellesley Pond, Morning Sun (1994). There were hundreds
of idea sketches for sculptures, some realized, others
remaining on paper as they were. In *The Death of Baby
Barn I* (1996), he'd sketched the dilapidated small barn

that had once stood along the road that led to our cottage. There had originally been three barns: we called them Mother, Father, and Baby. They marked the final stretch of the journey, just before we reached the lake. By the late nineties, only the smallest barn remained. Then, in time, its rafters folded, the roof collapsed, and it, too, sunk into the ground. Now, it's as if the barns were never there. But I know they were. When both my parents go, I alone will know the provenance and significance of this drawing's title. My siblings will, in turn, read the drawings in their own ways, drawn to different images which speak to the places of their history with my father, before I arrived and after.

In the second steel box, there was an impression he'd drawn from a window in a guest house in St. John's; my parents had been visiting me and my husband over the winter holiday in 2010 — a significant time, as together we waited for my first child to arrive. She was born on Boxing Day. Next, there was a quartet of four drawings from 1995: mounted grizzly-bear heads with the phrase "He killed the man who shot him" running above like a banner. This, too, was a reminder of a Christmas past, a holiday I'd spent with my parents at the Banff Centre for the Arts when I was a teenager. During the days, my mother had stayed in our room, writing, and my father had set up camp at the local museum, sketching taxidermy. He'd insisted that I accompany him for a tour one afternoon before the museum closed for the break. "Look at the bear!" he'd said, smiling brightly under the animal's cavernous open jaw. He was thrilled, too, by the stuffed moose head and its majestic antlers, sketches of which were also in the bank vault. I was a vegetarian then, unimpressed with dead animals, and somewhat embarrassed by how my father had practically moved into the museum for the week, although the director seemed pleased by the attention. There were few visitors over the afternoon that my father showed me around the glass cases, pointing out the glassy-eyed animals within.

There were hundreds of drawings in the bank vault that had been inspired by the rural Irish landscape where my parents had lived. I recognized the hump of the local mountain, the overgrown road to Sneem, the metal fence that kept cows from entering the yard. In a drawing from 1996 I saw the disintegrating chaise longue that had existed, for too long, at our cottage, a plastic floral cushion where generations of family had sunned themselves to a deep brown, when tanning was still fashionable. There was a rusted iron gate, threaded through with long grasses, that he'd drawn in Flavigny-sur-Ozerain, the medieval French village where we'd lived when I was three. There were pollarded trees from France and the weeping willows of our backyard in southwestern Ontario, as well as Spanish trees with no foliage, maybe from the year he'd spent living in the small fishing village with his first wife and my two older sisters, the community that had been so changed by tourism. There was a series of sketched palm trees and tropical plants, done in the late seventies during a vacation to Jamaica he'd taken with my mother, my two older sisters, and me. I was just over a year old, and still napping. My father stayed back with me during the afternoons while I slept, and my mother and sisters went to the beach. Our hotel room was on the ground floor, and the open porch provided a window into the island's plant life. Landscape, the natural world—this was the connecting thread that wove itself through all of my father's works. The places changed, sometimes drastically, but his enthusiasm for drawing the earth before him was unwavering.

In all, there were close to a thousand drawings stored in the vault. A collection spanning seven decades, a physical manifestation of time and study. We hadn't come close to exploring them all—the earlier works would be left to another day. These were not quick sketches. Or, they were, initially, but then they rotated through the corkboards of my father's life. In this way, they represented the work being done while looking, and while not looking, when his back was turned, when the good fairy visited. In the last box we explored, I discovered the crisscrossed fence-inspired drawings that I'd watched my dad unpin from his corkboard two years ago, when their purpose had finally taken shape.

Art is richer, more layered, and wiser than what we see in our textbooks, or on the walls of galleries. Every drawing housed in the beige walls of the bank informed the work that followed; each one, a problem solved, allowed my father to move forward. His later works were significant for all the practice, all the solutions, that had come before.

WHEN I'D VISITED MY FATHER's friend Hugh Mackenzie in the care home where he lived, he'd shown me a small oil painting, a reclining nude, which he'd done recently.

"I don't think I'm supposed to be using oil in this place," he'd said, shrugging.

"But where did you paint this?" I asked. "Do they offer life drawing classes here?"

"Oh God, no," he'd said, and laughed. "I don't need a model. I've drawn the human figure so many times in my life that now I do it from memory."

Then he'd told me an anecdote about one of American artist Edward Hopper's final paintings, *Sun in an Empty Room*. Hugh said that Hopper stared at a blank canvas for months before picking up his brush, and then painted the work from an image in his head. Hopper imagined the painting into being. It was not drawn from life, not a room he could return to and inspect; it was a room of his imagination and experience, and of his lifelong relationship to light and shadow and to space, both interior and exterior. Through the window we catch a glimpse of a treed thicket, the hint of wind in the branches, shut out by the panes of glass. There are impossible lines, and the trim appears only in the sections illuminated by the sun, and in this, the rules of perspective are somewhat askew, slightly and intentionally off, adding to the mystery of the emptiness.

I hadn't seen Hopper's painting, so the room I conjured as Hugh described the piece — the light, the
angles, the haunting mood — was Hugh's former studio.
The third-floor attic with its sloped ceiling and window
facing south, a shaft of light warming the wooden
floorboards. The cracks on the ceiling, the smudges
on the walls where he'd inadvertently rested a charcoal-
covered palm. Missing from this scene was his stool,
propped close to his easel, where, when I'd visited once
in my twenties, I'd seen his painting of two crouch-
ing women framed in an earthy brown, human forms
against the dark. Gone was his messy, paper-stacked
desk, and the postcards sent by artist friends during
their travels, some from my father. Gone was the lamp
that illuminated his canvases, and the paintings, stacked
against the wall and into the next room, once the bedroom of a child now grown and gone — the paintings
that had rested there en route to the gallery, also gone.

Sifting through my father's drawings at the bank that
day, I thought about Hopper's *Sun in an Empty Room*,
and the story that Hugh had told about the artist sitting
in front of his blank canvas until the painting revealed
itself. I thought about how Hugh no longer needed
to work from a life-drawing model. All three artists,
in their old age, were able to draw on their internal
resources, all those years of visual study, to produce
their work. "The creative part is one of the last things
to go," Hugh had said.

It was growing late and my father seemed tired. We
couldn't see the contents of every box in the vault that

day. We planned to return the following afternoon. I understood my father's need to revisit the bank, weekly, daily, to see his drawings. They represented his entire life: not just his output, but the places he'd visited, his family life, his various homes and studios, his earliest marks on paper, and his latest.

I RETURNED TO MY parents' home the next morning. It was the first spring day that I could go outside without a jacket. Earlier, I'd watched a robin making her nest. The world was still leafless and brown but there were tiny green shoots pushing their way up through the earth. The winter ice, that endless shield, had finally thawed. My mother was hosting a seventieth birthday party for her cousin Roseanne, and the living room was buzzing with women relatives, conversations stretching back seven decades.

I'd stopped in to say hello, but mostly I was there to pick up my father. We had a date to return to the bank vault.

"Go find your father," my mother said when I arrived.

First, I checked his drawing room, but he wasn't there. I stopped for a moment, as I nearly always do, to examine the space. The piano—top up, sheet music open. Drawings covered the surface of every table. Framed in the window was the postcard of Delacroix's boat that my dad had bought after we'd seen the show at the Metropolitan Museum of Art in New York the previous fall. He'd returned to the image and was reworking the sketches he'd done in the hotel room. In one, he'd filled the boat with a riot of colour so that it no longer looked like a vessel; instead, it was amoeba-like, although I saw a hint of the water in the bottom left, a rippled yellow and blue. In the second, he'd played with the boards of the hull, alternating colours — several bands of fuchsia, some pale yellows. Again, there was a hint of water, ripples along the side, but the boat's shape was flattened, splayed open, like a crushed seed. Along what would have been the starboard side of the hull he'd written "boat" in small red letters, crediting his inspiration.

I looked past the postcard of the boat and out to the barn, that relic of times past, the interior returned now to the birds, the neighbourhood cats fighting with raccoons, the voracious mice. I remembered the humid afternoon only a handful of years before when my husband, sister, brother-in-law, and I carried the art of my father's that had been stored there, on the second floor, down the stairs, across the lawn, then up the back staircase of my parents' home, where it would be safe in the dryness of the newly renovated section of their attic. I remembered the weight of the art, heavy in my arms on that summer's day. The endless stairs, the art secured, the weight lifted, for now.

This had marked one in a series of legacy-building events that were ongoing, and would continue, as the responsibility of my father's art fell to me and my siblings. The previous winter, my brother Aidan had spent two weekends alone with my father, beginning the process of cataloguing his works on paper. Over the previous two years, two of my father's large oil paintings had been acquired by provincial galleries. The first was the red *King and Queen*, which was now in the Winnipeg Art Gallery's permanent collection. The second was *Allegory*, which had finally been acquired by the Art Gallery of Ontario. The curator who'd halted the process had quit his job. The next person in line had carried on with the original acquisition. I imagine that, for my father, having his paintings secured was a little like knowing your children were settled, in life and love, as you aged into your later years.

Next, I checked the side living room where my father rested in the late mornings or afternoons, his headphones on, listening to classical music or reading a book. He'd been reading a biography of the Roosevelts during their time at the White House, and the hardcover lay face-down on the coffee table, opened to his page, but he was not there. The couch held only his impression in its cushions. I climbed the stairs and checked the second-floor bedrooms, the bathrooms, and, although he never spent time in there, I also checked the back room on the first floor that my mother used as her writing studio. He was not in there, of course, and there was no indication that he'd been anywhere in the house, with the exception of his imprint in the couch cushions and the book he'd left in the living room. It seemed strange. Had he gone out, I wondered? He often walked across the road to the grocery store, or down the hill to the main street to visit the post office, the drugstore, and, of course, the bank. A hum of panic underpinned my search, familiar from two months before when my mother had called me in Ireland to tell me that my father was in hospital.

For a time, after my father's surgery, we believed that if you fixed the heart, ordered its beat, set it neatly in place and on track, the mind would follow suit. It must have been the heart, for those months, that had caused confusions for my father, more bad days than good. It had been blocked, with a sloth-like beat, barely registering, and now, here he was on the other side. Alert, focused, tired, yes, but surrounded by the regularity of his world, his space, his artist's tools; trapped inside by the winter's endless ice, a new climate in a world that was failing, he was content, had returned to his drawing table as if nothing had happened. People stopped in and remarked on his good nature, on his clear mind. It was as if the sun had risen, burned away the fog, and lit the landscapes in the foreground of his mind, and also what lay in the distance.

Maybe this was only the perception of those closest to my father, but perception—and, in turn, how we interact with the aging among us, how we treat people with dementia—affects how they perceive themselves. A slight lift of concern could change the measure of a room. It could lift him, and us. I knew it was possible that we were engaging in an optimistic group delusion but I also didn't care.

I came back through the kitchen—even checking the walk-in pantry for my father, who has never cooked in his life—and arrived back in the main living room where I'd started. The party had grown. Distracted, I said hello to the newly arrived cousins, but I didn't linger.

"I can't find Dad," I whispered to my mother. "He's not in his drawing room or anywhere else. Could he be outside?"

"Check the studio," she said.

It was the last place I looked, but it was also the most obvious. I opened the back door and there was my dad, paintbrush in hand, working on a 3-by-2-foot painting that was propped on his desk and leaning against the wall, his easel having been misplaced sometime over the months that he'd abandoned this space.

"I thought you said it was too cold to work in the studio, Dad."

"Oh, really? No, it's not bad."

He'd either forgotten saying this, or he'd changed his mind.

"Let me just show you something," he said. "It's almost finished, but I don't quite know what it needs yet."

He showed me a horizontal painting in a pale-pink frame. On the right side of the canvas, there was a tall, narrow doorway that reminded me of his *Threshold* paintings from the eighties — all those towering, upright open graves. Along the top there was a land-scape that looked like the vista that revealed itself when you crested the hill on the way to the cottage, and, for just a second, perspective askew, the lake appeared above the trees as if it were the sky. A series of angles receded into the distance, and there was a small green box, centre right. Pale bands of vertical colour ran along the left side, which was less detailed.

"The idea is that one side of the painting is moderately realistic and also the shapes are defined, and then they gradually go off to this side where you're not sure what it is," he said, sweeping his hand from right to left across the canvas. "It's like it's unfinished, that side, but that's part of the problem that I wanted to try. Could you do a painting with high finish and then gradually let it fade out the other side?"

I turned my attention to a second painting that was sitting on the floor, propped up by a row of cupboards. It was dark green, also abstract, and looked as if he'd drawn across the paint with some kind of crayon.

"Is this also new?"

"It is, this one is my latest. It's in oil, but the richer colours are acrylic stick."

"What is this?" I pointed to what looked like fragments of his signature encased in barbed wire, down in the bottom-left corner of the painting.

"Oh, that?" he said. "I can't even write my own name."

He did not sound bothered by this admission. He'd accepted this new hurdle. He'd return to it later, on another day, when it came easier to him. The signature was uninteresting to my father. It was the painting that drew his focus, as has always been the case. I noticed, too, that the date in the bottom-right corner was strange. It seemed to have been painted in 6019 — he'd mixed up the numbers six and two—painted in some futuristic year, far from now, that neither of us would ever see. I didn't point this out. Taking his lead, I thought, *Oh, that?* He would change the date, too, when needed.

Roseanne opened the door to the studio.

"Just saying hello to Tony," she said, embracing my dad. Then she turned to me.

"I read your article," she said, referencing a magazine article I'd written about my father the previous year. "It made me cry and I wanted to tell you that you worry too much about your dad. I tried to call you, to tell you that you didn't need to worry about him. He's doing great. You just need to keep interviewing him now."

The previous winter Roseanne had called and left me a long voice message about how it was my duty to record the history of Canadian art that my father has stored in his memory. Roseanne has an affinity for the long-ago, its people and in particular its artifacts. She collects and sells history's objects—buttons, jewellery, furniture—sometimes showing her wares at markets, sometimes in pop-up stores that she creates with other vendors. I'd once visited her home and found her entrance hall lined with antique dressers, some stacked two or three high, tower-like. She couldn't bear to part with them. The past is her country and she knows it well. I knew I'd be wise to listen to anything she had to say on the topic, and yet, in the whorl of midlife and small children and endless dinners and school forms and various work contracts and holidays and dreary domestic duties, I'd forgotten to call her back.

I'd seen Roseanne six months later at an outdoor flea market hosted in the park of the small town where my parents live. She was packing her trunk full of unsold wares from her stall, and when she spotted me, she looked panicked. She didn't ask me about my children or even myself, but instead picked up where her voice-mail had left off.

"You must do it now," she'd said, her pale eyes wide. She lived near my parents, and saw them often. In her constant search for pieces of the past, she often turned up items of interest for my father—antique keys, handmade wooden trinkets, old farm equip-ment—some of which he'd used in his boxes. I felt bad for not returning her call, and told her so, but she brushed my apologies away. I hadn't understood her intensity on the phone, and was reluctant to acknow-ledge her message on that day at the park, too. She was telling me something I didn't want to hear, and, like an obstinate child, I didn't listen.

There in my father's studio I recalled that conversa-tion six months ago, and how I'd seen her imperative, that I record my father's stories, as a warning. I realized, now, that she'd hoped I would talk to my dad about the past because he was a repository, not a drying well. I should have called her back when she'd left the message. I'd misunderstood her point.

Roseanne left to re-join her birthday party and I watched my dad wipe the paint from his brush on a paper towel, then reach for the turpentine to clean his hands. He wasn't wearing his painter's jacket with its shiny colour smears, only his regular clothes, a brown sweater over a collared shirt. I realized that he hadn't planned to paint that morning—but there was a problem he was trying to solve, and, as the party guests arrived and filled out the living room, he'd slipped quietly into his back-room studio to untangle it.

A YEAR AGO, I asked my father why he made art.

"You get up in the morning, you make breakfast, you make art."

Art was his life's focus, and while there's no cure for aging, studies have found that having a reason to get up in the morning, what the Japanese call *ikigai*—which is the confluence of what you love, what the world needs, what can support you financially, and what you're good at—is associated with decreased mortality and better physical and mental health in old age. People in Japan live longer than in nearly anywhere else in the world, in particular on the island of Okinawa, which ranks highest among the world's five "blue zones," the regions where people live the longest. The climate is good, the diet is healthy, people are physically active, but it's the concept of *ikigai*, and the continued work and associated feeling of usefulness, that has the greatest impact on mortality for islanders. Like my father, they do not recognize retirement.

"I just never stopped drawing," he told me. "I have been rewarded often enough that I'm still curious to see what would happen if I did one more."

There has never been an end for my father. He will work until he can no longer, because every time he starts a drawing, painting, or sculpture, he is always at the beginning of something new.

For many artists, there is no final work, or their body of work is infinite because it never quite feels finished. My father has laid paintings to rest for decades before returning to finish them. The rose tondo, called *Flowers in Pink* (2010), started in the mid-sixties, is an example. In the 1970s, not long after my parents met, my father spied a storage opportunity on his future in-laws' property — the wooden barn that now sits outside the window of his drawing room. He was living in a townhouse then, crowded with his teenaged daughters, and had no extra room for art. He stacked seven of the large, round paintings on Masonite in what was once a horse's stall. Forty years later, as my mother rooted out the storm windows for the home, which they'd purchased after my grandmother's death, she discovered that the panes were buttressed by round, pressure-treated pieces of wood. On a hunch, using the sleeve of her jacket, she rubbed a small area free of dirt. There were brush-strokes underneath.

My grandmother's handyman had placed the paintings between the storm windows, likely as a means of protecting the glass. If my parents hadn't purchased the home, it's possible a new owner might have made the same discovery and understood the work's value; but they might just as easily have rented a dumpster and tossed the paintings, along with the rest of the

accumulated detritus: the scrap wood, the filing cabinets, the antique scythe, and the pioneer plough.

It was late fall, and my parents wheeled the enormous paintings out of the barn and into the morning
light. They dusted all seven, revealing the abstract landscapes beneath. Afterwards, my father propped each
painting on an easel in his studio for a time and studied
the marks of his younger self. By afternoon he'd started
adding to the works, taking up where he'd left off more
than forty years before.

We look for messages in an artist's finale, but, for
many, pinpointing an artist's last work is impossible, as
Leonard Cohen's editors discovered when tasked with
arranging the chronology of his final works of poetry
and prose for his posthumous collection, *The Flame*.
Cohen had been consulted on the selections, understanding this would be his last book, so he must have
known, to some extent, that these works were complete. But he was a revisionist, and could work on the
same poem over periods of time that lasted from years
to decades. This might be why, even in consultation,
he didn't give any clue as to how to order the book.
"It would be challenging — if not impossible — to
proceed chronologically," wrote Robert Faggen and
Alexandra Pleshoyano in their editorial note. "Leonard
would often work in the same notebooks over many
years with various coloured inks showing the different
entries." Which colour came first, which came last,
remains a mystery.

WE PLANNED TO LEAVE the house to the gathered women for the afternoon, return to the bank vault. My father wanted me to know what was in there because at some point, along with my siblings, it would become my responsibility. That time still felt far off, but I also felt ready to step into the role. In some ways, I'd been building up to it my entire life.

"There's no rush," I said, standing back to look at the painting propped on his easel. "If you want to keep working."

"No, it's okay," he said, placing the cleaned brush in a coffee tin and taking my arm. "I'll get back to it later."

I thought of my mother's words at my father's bedside in the hospital.

He has more work to do.

And he did.

When the revelation of my dad's memory problems had first surfaced, an old worry had seeped back into the foreground of my thoughts. It was a familiar, unsettling feeling, one fuelled by my insatiable need to research—reading the cruel words of critics concerning de Kooning, studying the visual collapse of self in the progressive portraits of William Utermohlen. But my father was neither of those artists. He could only ever be himself. He'd not been devastated by the diagnosis. In fact, he'd been relieved to have a name to place on his troubling memory issues. Also, my father's mind had always worked differently. He lived in a sideways drift. He was there and also not there. He was making art even if he was passing through the living room on his way to the front door, leaving for work at the university, or as he ferried me from our rented home in a medieval Burgundian village to my preschool in the next town. He thought about art as he ate, reflecting, unconsciously, on his own work, pinned in front of him. He had always lived in the world and outside of it, operating, often, with a level of remove that could not be permeated by details of the everyday. The name of my high school boyfriend, the street address of my closest friend who lived in the same small town as my family, the details of my childhood doctor and dentist appointments—these were left to my mother to organize and remember. He simply couldn't hold on to this information, and now, he no longer had to. He was free to focus on the world of his art, pushing forward, his urge to create unbroken.

Epilogue: Sunset

MY FATHER WAS VISITING, and we were out for a walk with the dog. It was early January 2020, and unseasonably warm. Water pooled along the sidewalk beneath our feet. There was some ice, so I took my father's arm. My mother was running errands. My children were at school, Andrew, at work. The morning was quiet. The dog stopped to sniff a crusted snowbank and we stopped with him. It had been nearly a year since my father had his pacemaker installed, and a few years since his doctor had raised the possibility of dementia. Time had moved on. We were speaking about the undergraduate course I'd recently started teaching. It was about writing, but visual art had crept in.

"I've been sharing images of artworks with my writing students."

"Which ones?"

"Mark Rothko's *Orange, Red, Yellow.*"

This was an abstract painting from the early sixties with hovering squares of colour, as bright and as startling as a hallucination. My father had known Rothko's work since he was a young art student.

"Sunset," my father said, which is how art writers often described the ethos of this piece. "Who else?"

"Morris Louis, his most famous one," I said, forgetting the title of the painting. Louis had been one of the earliest colour field painters, Rothko's contemporary.

My father paused, looked up at the sky, which was grey and without texture. Then he turned back to me.

"Mostly blank canvas, the lines of colour move in on the diagonal, from either side."

"Yes, that's the one."

I thought back to the previous month, when I'd accompanied my dad to visit his geriatrician. A nurse had administered a series of memory tests. In one, he was given a grouping of unrelated words to remember, *to hold on to*, she'd said. When asked to repeat the list of words a few minutes later, he'd shaken his head.

"It would just be a guess at this point."

And yet, today, on this dull, overcast morning, he pulled effortlessly from his image bank: *Sunset. Mostly blank canvas, the lines of colour move in on the diagonal, from either side.*

This was a different kind of art-viewing journey than we'd taken in the past. We walked slowly along the icy sidewalk, as if from painting to painting in an art gallery. There were no walls, only the crisp winter air, and yet, there we stood, side by side, conjuring the work as if it were in front of us, talking about art, as we'd always done.

Later in the day, my mother returned from running errands and Andrew came home from work. Our children, who'd been back from school for a few hours by then, were buzzing around the living room, seeking attention. A friend stopped by with her timid dog, and the animal skulked in the front entranceway. Our own mutt barked in at us through the glass of the back door, affronted by his exclusion. My father was sitting quietly on the couch. He caught my eye, pointed at the old war trunk that we used as a coffee table, the one he'd sketched while visiting us in Victoria for what was to become the electric-pink painting *Strong Box I*. He ran his hand along the corners, which were buffeted in metal, and across the worn leather and remnants of paint on its sides.

"Do you have a piece of paper?"

I knew what he wanted. Not office paper, something thicker. I found one of my daughter's old sketchbooks, and tore him out a single page.

"Do you need a pen?"

"No, I always have a few," he said, then fished three pens from his front pocket, chose one, and began to draw the war chest for the fifteenth, twentieth, maybe the thirtieth time since he'd first sketched it seven years before.

Both dogs were inside now. One snarled at the other. The conversation turned to architecture and heritage, and how property developers were erasing the past.

My daughter began playing the piano in the next room. My son, lying on the living room floor, was singing softly as he ran his toy cars along the carpet. In the centre, my father sat sketching, transported to that unreachable place, the landscape of his imagination, as life carried on all around him.

Notes

PROLOGUE: STILL LIFE

Fuchs, R. H. *Dutch Painting*. Toronto and New York: Oxford University Press, 1978.

Fiore, Julia. "The Hidden Secrets Lurking in Dutch Still Life Paintings." *Artsy*, September 4, 2018.

Gombrich, E. H. *The Story of Art*. New York: Phaidon, 1950.

Harris, Beth, and Steven Zucker, creators. "Willem Kalf, Still Life with a Silver Ewer" (video). Khan Academy. https://www.khanacademy.org/humanities/monarchy-enlightenment/baroque-art1/holland/v/kalf-ewer.

THE EARTH RETURNS TO LIFE

Vastokas, Joan. *Worlds Apart: The Symbolic Landscapes of Tony Urquhart* (catalogue). Art Gallery of Windsor, 1988.

Slivka, Rose. "Introduction" in *Elaine de Kooning: The Spirit of Abstract Expressionism, Selected Writings*. New York: George Braziller, 1994.

Stonard, John-Paul. "Abstract Expressionism: Not just macho heroes with brushes." *The Guardian*, September 3, 2016.

Leclerc, Denise. *The Crisis of Abstraction in Canada: The 1950s* (catalogue). National Gallery of Canada, Ottawa, 1992.

Lot 49: *The Earth Returns to Life*. Heffel Fine Art Auction House, Fall 2009. https://www.heffel.com/auction/Details_E.aspx?ID=18072.

Vastokas, Joan. *Dialogues of Reconciliation: The Imagination of Tony Urquhart*. Canadian Matrix Series, organized by the Meridian Gallery, San Francisco, and co-sponsored by the Art Gallery of Peterborough, Ontario, 1989.

Transforming Chronologies: An Atlas of Drawings, Part One (exhibition). January to April, 2006, Museum of Modern Art, New York.

Hughes, Robert. "Triumph of the will: He was old, deaf and virtually broke. But a new exhibition of Goya's last works shows that nothing could dampen his creative spirit." *The Guardian*, April 12, 2006.

Perkins, Cory. "How David Hockney Became the World's Foremost iPad Painter." *Wired*, November 18, 2013. https://www.wired.com/2013/11/hockney/.

Athill, Diana. *Somewhere Towards the End*. New York: Norton, 2009.

Angell, Roger. *This Old Man: All in Pieces*. New York: Penguin Random House, 2015.

Danchev, Alex. *Cezanne: A Life*. New York: Pantheon, 2012.

Bailey, Anthony. *Standing in the Sun: A Life of J. M. W. Turner*. New York: HarperCollins, 1997.

Hills, Patricia. *Alice Neel*. New York: Harry N. Abrams, 1983.

Quinn, Bridget. *Broad Strokes: 15 Women Who Made Art and Made History (In that Order)*. San Francisco: Chronicle Books, 2017.

Ehrlich White, Barbara. *Renoir: An Intimate Biography*. London: Thames & Hudson, 2017.

Munsterberg, Hugo. *The Crown of Life*. Boston: Harcourt, 1983.

Lindauer, Martin S. *Aging, Creativity, and Art: A Positive Perspective on Late-Life Development*. New York: Kluwer Academic, 2003.

Clark, Kenneth. "The Artist Grows Old." *Daedalus* 30:5 (2006): 77–90.

King, Ross. "Claude Monet and the Old Age Style." *Huffington Post*, March 2, 2019. https://www.huffingtonpost.ca/ross-king/claude-monet-water-lilies_b_15107052.html.

King, Ross. *Mad Enchantment: Claude Monet and the Painting of the Water Lilies*. Toronto: Anchor, 2017.

Munsterberg, Hugo. *The Crown of Life*.

Smiles, Sam. "Unfinished? Repulsive? Or the work of a prophet?: Late Turner." *Tate Etc.* 15 (Spring 2009). http://www.tate.org.uk/context-comment/articles/unfinished-repulsive-or-work-prophet.

Aronson, Louise. *Elderhood: Redefining Aging, Transforming Medicine, Reimagining Life*. New York: Bloomsbury, 2019.

Rowe, J. W., and R. L. Kahn. *Successful Aging*. New York: Pantheon, 1998.

Krystal, Arthur. "Old News: Why can't we tell the truth about aging?" *The New Yorker*, November 4, 2019.

Hill, Kelly. "Senior Artists in Canada" (report). Hill Strategies Research, 2010. https://hillstrategies.com/wp-content/uploads/1970/01/Senior_Artists_full_report.pdf.

White, Tracie. "Eye diseases changed great painters' vision of their work later in their lives." *Stanford Report*, April 2007. https://news.stanford.edu/news/2007/april11/med-optart-041107.html.

Ehrlich White. *Renoir.*

Levin, Gail. *Lee Krasner: A Biography.* New York: HarperCollins, 2011.

Utermohlen, Pat. "William Utermohlen." September 2006. https://www.williamutermohlen.org/index.php/9-about/essays/4-pat-2006.

Hester, Micaela (Public Relations Program Manager, Georgia O'Keeffe Museum, Santa Fe). Personal correspondence with author, May 19, 2017.

Drohojowska-Philp, Hunter. *Full Bloom: The Art and Life of Georgia O'Keeffe.* New York: W. W. Norton, 2005.

Kastenbaum, Robert. "The Creative Impulse: Why It Won't Just Quit." *Generations: Journal of the American Society on Aging* 15:2 (Spring 1991): 7–12.

KING AND QUEEN

Simonton, Dean Keith. "The Swan-Song Phenomenon: Last-works effects for 172 classical composers." *Psychology of Aging* 4:1 (March 1989): 42–47.

King, Ross. Interview with author. April 17, 2017.

Kardosh, Robert (Director, Marion Scott Gallery, Vancouver). Interviews with author. June–October 2017.

Mackenzie, Hugh. *Show 88* (exhibition). Bau-xi Gallery, Toronto, September 10–22, 2016. www.bau-xi.com/blogs/exhibitions/hugh-mackenzie-show-88.

Urquhart, Emily. "Portrait of the Artist as Father," in Sandra Martin, ed., *The First Man in My Life: Daughters Write About Fathers.* Toronto: Penguin, 2007: 227–238.

CORKBOARD

Tony Urquhart: Twenty-Five Years: Retrospective (exhibition). Kitchener-Waterloo Art Gallery, 1978.

"Yesterday." *The Beatles Bible.* https://www.beatlesbible.com/songs/yesterday/. Accessed December 16, 2019.

Ehrenzweig, Anton. *The Hidden Order of Art.* Berkeley: University of California Press, 1967.

Lehman, Harvey C. *Age and Achievement.* Philadelphia: American Philosophical Society, 1953.

Lehman, Harvey C. "More About Age and Achievement." *The Gerontologist* 2:3: 141–148.

Smith, Henry D. *Hokusai: 100 Views of Mount Fuji.* New York: George Braziller, 2000.

Carson, Shelley. "Creativity and the Aging Brain." *Psychology Today,* March 30, 2009. https://www.psychologytoday.com/ca/blog/life-art/200903/creativity-and-the-aging-brain/.

Simonton, Dean Keith. "Creativity in the Later Years: Optimistic Prospects for Achievement." *The Gerontological Society of America* 30:5 (1990): 626–631.

Cohen, Gene D. "The Impact of Professionally Conducted Cultural Programs on Older Adults" (National Endowment for the Arts Creativity and Aging Study: Final Report). April 2006. https://www.americansforthearts.org/node/100548.

Freundlich, Alfred, and John Shiveley. "Creativity and the Exceptional Aging Artist." *Clinical Interventions in Aging* 1:2 (June 2006): 197–200.

Galenson, David. "The Two Life Cycles of Human Creativity" (Research summary). *National Bureau of Economic Research Reporter,* Fall 2003. https://www.nber.org/reporter/fall03/galenson.html.

Galenson, David. *Old Masters and Young Geniuses: The Two Life Cycles of Human Creativity*. Princeton, N.J.: Princeton University Press, 2007.

Andersson, E., et al. "Creativity in Old Age: A Longitudinal Study." *Aging* 1:2 (1989): 159–64.

Salat, David H., et al. "Thinning of the Cerebral Cortex in Aging." *Cerebral Cortex* 14:7 (2004): 721–730.

Marmour, M. F. "Ophthalmology and Art: Simulation of Monet's Cataracts and Degas' Retinal Disease." *Archives of Ophthalmology* 124:12 (December 2006): 1764–1769.

White, Tracie. "Eye diseases changed great painters' vision of their work later in their lives." *Stanford Report*, April 11, 2007. https://news.stanford.edu/news/2007/april11/med-optart-041107.html.

Said-Metwaly, Sameh. "Approaches to Measuring Creativity: A Systematic Literature Review." *Creativity* 4:2 (2017): 238–275.

Henry, Martha. Interview with the author. July 24, 2018.

Galenson, David. Interviews with author. May 11, 2017 and July 2017.

Clark, Kenneth. "The Artist Grows Old." *Daedalus* 30:5 (2006): 77–90.

Said, Edward. *On Late Style: Music and Literature Against the Grain*. New York: Vintage, 2007.

Cole, Thomas R., and Mary G. Winkler. *The Oxford Book of Aging: Reflections on the Journey of Life*. Oxford: Oxford University Press, 1994.

HOUSE AMONG TREES

Transforming Chronologies: An Atlas of Drawings, Part One (exhibition). Museum of Modern Art, New York, Jan 26–Apr 24, 2006. https://www.moma.org/calendar/exhibitions/87?locale=en.

World Health Organization. "Ten Facts on Dementia." Updated September 2019. https://www.who.int/features/factfiles/dementia/en/.

The Alzheimer's Association. "Alzheimer's Facts and Figures." https://www.alz.org/alzheimers-dementia/facts-figures. Accessed March 20, 2020.

World Health Organization. *Global Action Plan on the Public Health Response to Dementia 2017–2025*. Geneva: World Health Organization, 2017.

Forsyth, Alex, et al. "What Paint Can Tell Us: A Fractal Analysis of Neurological Changes in Seven Artists." *Neuropsychology* 31:1 (2017): 1–10.

Utermohlen, Pat. "William Utermohlen." September 2006. https://www.williamutermohlen.org/index.php/9-about/essays/4-pat-2006.

Stevens, Mark, and Annalyn Swan. *de Kooning: An American Master*. New York: Knopf, 2004.

Miller, Bruce, et al. "Portraits of Artists: Emergence of Visual Creativity in Dementia." *Neurological Review* 61 (June 2004).

Espinel, Carlos Hugo. "de Kooning's late colours and forms: dementia, creativity, and the healing powers of art." *The Lancet* 347 (1996): 1096–1098.

Willem de Kooning: The Late Paintings, the 1980s (exhibition). The Museum of Modern Art (New York), January 26–April 29, 1997. https://www.moma.org/calendar/exhibitions/233?locale=en.

Vogel, Carol. "De Kooning Intrigue Lives On." *New York Times*, October 6, 1997.

Tompkins, Calvin. "De Kooning as Melodrama." *The New Yorker*, February 10, 1997.

Storr, R. "At last light," in J. Jenkins, ed., *Willem de Kooning: The Late Paintings, the 1980s*. Minneapolis: Walker Art Center and San Francisco Museum of Modern Art, 1995: 39–79.

Tully, Judd. "Abstract Expressionism Leads Sotheby's Contemporary Sale in New York, with $30.1 M. Willem de Kooning Topping Market-Affirming $270.7 M. Total." *ARTnews*, November 15, 2019. https://www. artnews.com/art-news/market/sothebys-de-kooning-contemporary-auction-13582/.

Glover, Michael. "Late flowering or failing: Did work by artists like De Kooning, Renoir, Matisse and Monet decline in old age?" *The Independent*, October 10, 2017.

Kontos, Pia. "'The painterly hand': embodied consciousness and Alzheimer's disease." *Journal of Aging Studies* 17 (2003), 151–170.

Carlson, Joan Tyor. "AD Visits: Willem de Kooning." *Architectural Digest*, September 1, 2011. https://www.architecturaldigest.com/gallery/willem-de-kooning-hamptons-home-studio-slideshow.

UNTITLED

Stanley Spencer (exhibition). Art Gallery of Ontario, September 14–December 30, 2001. https://ago.ca/exhibitions/stanley-spencer.

Siegel, Alisa. *Life, Still: The Unbuttoning of Christiane Pflug* (radio documentary.) CBC Radio, posted May 1, 2015. https://www.cbc.ca/radio/thesundayedition/men-will-be-boys-the-refugee-problem-christiana-pflug-ve-day-1.3055705/life-still-the-unbuttoning-of-christiane-pflug-1.3055731.

Davis, Ann. *Somewhere Waiting: The Life and Art of Christiane Pflug*. Toronto: Oxford University Press, 1991.

"Christine Pflug, 1936–1972" (website). http://www.christianepflug.com/.

Lindauer, Martin S. "Old Age Style" (encyclopedia entry), in Steven Pritzker, ed., *Encyclopedia of Creativity*. Academic Press (Elsevier), 1999.

Lindauer, Martin S. *Aging, Creativity and Art: A Positive Perspective on Late-Life Development*. New York: Kluwer Academic, 2003.

"Is this the last ever painting by Jackson Pollock?" *Phaidon*, August 29, 2012. https://ca.phaidon.com/agenda/art/articles/2012/august/29/is-this-the-last-ever-painting-by-jackson-pollock/.

"The final days of Jackson Pollock." *Phaidon*, August 11, 2014. https://ca.phaidon.com/agenda/art/articles/2014/august/11/the-final-days-of-jackson-pollock/.

Urquhart, Tony. *The Revenants: Long Shadows* (catalogue). Waterloo: University of Waterloo Art Gallery, 2002.

Watch This Space: Contemporary Art from the AGO Collection (exhibition), 2013. https://ago.ca/exhibitions/watch-space-contemporary-art-ago-collection.

Quinn, Bridget. *Broad Strokes: 15 Women Who Made Art and Made History (In that Order)*. San Francisco: Chronicle Books, 2017.

Hills, Patricia. *Alice Neel*. New York: Harry N. Abrams, 1983.

Temkin, Ann, and Richard Flood. *Alice Neel*. New York: Harry N. Abrams (in association with the Philadelphia Museum of Art), 2000.

"*The Raft of the Medusa.*" *The Louvre Notices*. Paris, Musée du Louvre, 2010. https://www.louvre.fr/en/oeuvre-notices/raft-medusa.

Stokstad, Marilyn. "The Romanticism of Géricault and Delacroix." *Art History: Volume Two*. New York: Prentice Hall, 1995: 960–962.

Harris, Beth, and Steven Zucker, creators. "Géricault, *Raft of the Medusa*" (video). Kahn Academy. https://www.khanacademy.org/humanities/becoming-modern/romanticism/romanticism-in-france/v/g-ricault-raft-of-the-medusa-1818-19.

The Long Run (exhibition). Museum of Modern Art (New York), November 11, 2017–May 5, 2018. https://www.moma.org/calendar/exhibitions/3879.

Sacks, Oliver. *Everything in its Place: First Loves and Lost Tales.* New York: Knopf, 2019.

de Beauvoir, Simone. *The Coming of Age.* New York: Penguin, 1972.

ARTICULATED LAIR

"Jay Moss." http://www.carterburdengallery.org/jay-moss.

Gonzalez, David. "Late Bloomer finds audience for his art." *New York Times,* November 30, 2014.

Moss, Jordan. "69 years After the War, an Artist Makes Another Debut." *The Forward,* November 30, 2014.

Bruce Nauman: Disappearing Acts (exhibition). Museum of Modern Art (New York), October 21, 2018–February 25, 2019. https://www.moma.org/calendar/exhibitions/3852.

"Louise Bourgeois." Museum of Modern Art (New York). https://www.moma.org/artists/710.

Rosenberg, Karen. "A 101-Year-Old Artist Finally Gets Her Due at the Whitney." *New York Times,* September 15, 2016.

Sontag, Deborah. "At 94, Carmen Herrera Is Art's Hot New Thing, and Enjoying It." *New York Times,* December 19, 2009.

Cohen, Claire. "OWAS: Meet the Grand Dames of the Art World." *The Telegraph,* April 25, 2013.

Sussman, Anna Louie. "Why Old Women Have Replaced Young Men as the Art World's Darlings." *Artsy,* June 19, 2017.

Schultz, Abby. "Female Artists' Works on the Rise." *Penta*, June 20, 2018. www.barrons.com/articles/female-artists-works-on-the-rise-1529467305.

Gavin, Francesca. "The Rise of the Older Woman Artist: How a Generation of Female Artists Are Finally Getting Their Due." *Sleek*, October 4, 2017. www.sleek-mag.com/article/older-women-artists/.

Gnyp, Marta. "Miraculous Resurrections: The contemporary art market of older and deceased women artists" (lecture). University of Loughborough, UK: Association of Art Historians Conference, April 6–8, 2017. www.martagnyp.com/articles/miraculous-resurrections-the-contemporary-art-market-of-older-and-deceased-women-artists.php.

Greer, Germaine. "Who is Britain's hottest new artist? A 76-year-old called Rose Wylie." *The Guardian*, July 9, 2010.

Sherwin, Skye. "Rose Wylie: 'I want to be known for my paintings, not because I'm old.'" *The Guardian*, November 22, 2017.

Saner, Emer. "Rose Wylie: 'My mother thought women should have an escape route.'" *The Guardian*, February 13, 2012.

STARRY NIGHT(S)

"Margaret Atwood reads Mavis Gallant" (podcast). *The New Yorker*, April 1, 2013. https://www.newyorker.com/books/page-turner/fiction-podcast-margaret-atwood-reads-mavis-gallant.

Sampson, Denis. "Mavis Gallant's 'Voices Lost in Snow': The Origins of Fiction." *Journal of the Short Story in English* 42 (Spring 2004): 135–145.

Moffat, John. Interview with author, Wednesday, October 3, 2018.

de Leeuw, Ronald, ed., and Arnold Pomerans, trans. *The Letters of Vincent Van Gogh*. London: Penguin, 1996.

Lochnan, Katharine, ed. *Mystical Landscapes: From Vincent van Gogh to Emily Carr*. London and New York: Prestel, 2016.

THE RUNNER

Mouly, Françoise. 'Bruce McCall's Gluten-Free-Gluten.' *The New Yorker*, April 2, 2018.

Mouly, Françoise. "Cover Story: 'Glass Houses,' by Bruce McCall." *The New Yorker*, October 31, 2016.

McCall, Bruce, and David Letterman. *This Land Was Made for You and Me (But Mostly Me): Billionaires in the Wild.* New York: Blue Rider Press, 2013.

McCall, Bruce. *Thin Ice: Coming of Age in Canada.* New York: Vintage, 2013.

Bruce McCall, "What is retro futurism?" (TEDTalk). "Serious Play" Art Center Design Conference, Pasadena, C.A., 2008. https://www.ted.com/talks/bruce_mccall_what_is_retro_futurism.

Delacroix (exhibition). Metropolitan Museum of Art (New York), September 17, 2018–January 6, 2019.

Strickland, Eliza. "The Most Dangerous Muse: Parkinson's Gave her the Gift of Creativity." *Nautilus*, September 6, 2018. http://nautil.us/issue/64/the-unseen/the-most-dangerous-muse-rp.

Pollitt, Katha. "Lilacs in September." *The New Yorker*, September 14, 2003.

CROSS-STITCH

Hague, Matthew. "Designing for dementia: Long-term memory care, from the ground up." *Globe and Mail*, August 11, 2019.

Levin, Gail. *Lee Krasner: A Biography.* New York: HarperCollins, 2011.

THE WRECK OF HOPE

Lorimer, Hayden. "Why ice is our greatest emotional landscape." *The Guardian*, December 19, 2015.

SUN IN AN EMPTY ROOM

Cohen, Leonard. *The Flame: Poems and Selections from Notebooks.* Robert Faggen and Alexandra Pleshoyano, eds. Toronto: McClelland and Stewart, 2018.

García, Héctor, and Francesc Miralles. *Ikigai: The Japanese Secret to a Long and Happy Life.* New York: Penguin, 2017.

EPILOGUE: SUNSET

Teodorczuk, Tom. "£53.9m Rothko sunset leads the way at record modern art sale." *Go London*, May 9, 2012. https://www.standard.co.uk/go/london/exhibitions/539m-rothko-sunset-leads-the-way-at-record-modern-art-sale-7728426.html.

Waters, Florence. "Why Mark Rothko is Still Setting Records." *The Telegraph*, May 9, 2012. https://www.telegraph.co.uk/culture/art/9254687/Why-Mark-Rothko-is-still-setting-records.html.

Acknowledgements

SARAH MACLACHLAN CALLED ME on a Friday afternoon
and made me believe I could write this book. She's a
fierce champion and her confidence in me buoyed me
through this project. I'm grateful to her for this. I'm
thankful to Janie Yoon and Michelle MacAleese, the
keen, gentle, brilliant editors who worked on this manu-
script and helped with various neuroses (mine) along
the way. I'm indebted to Melanie Little for her copy-
editing wizardry and to Gemma Wain for her close and
thoughtful proofread of this text. I'm grateful to Alysia
Shewchuk for a cover design that fills my heart with joy
every time I see it, and to Maria Golikova for her kind
and organized way of moving the book-making process
along; to Curtis Samuel and Joshua Greenspon for their
early enthusiasm in promoting this book, and to the
rest of the team at House of Anansi Press. After meeting everyone and seeing their cool office, I wondered if

maybe they had an opening that I could fill so I could go there every day.

My agent, Sam Haywood, is tireless. (Actually, I do wonder if she sleeps.) She has been supportive since we first connected over busy lives with small children and a shared love of literature. I'm grateful to have her in my life.

It was five years ago that I approached Carmine Starnino at *The Walrus* magazine with my story idea that creativity doesn't nosedive in old age. Rather than run screaming, Carmine was fully on board and helped to shape the article that this book grew into, as did Daniel Viola, through his insightful edits on each of my subsequent drafts of the piece. I was fortunate to work with both of them and everybody at The Walrus.

I am grateful to the Chawkers Foundation Writers Project for supporting The Walrus Books and making it possible for writers to take the time to engage with the ideas that matter most to Canadians. It is a true gift. This book would not exist without this initiative.

I'M THANKFUL TO Carrie Snyder and Tasneem Jamal for their presence in my life and for their influence on this work. It was our Friday morning writing group meetings that steered this ship to port—rather than off course—and I'm grateful to both of them for writerly and moral support all the way through.

Nothing would be possible without my husband, Andrew Trant. He understood that I needed to write this book better than I did, and I'm grateful, every day, to have him by my side. My kids are adorable and they did nothing to help me write this book, but they did survive days without me when I had to disappear to work, and apparently they are better-behaved when I'm not around, so I guess I'm grateful for that. I'm thankful to my in-laws, Don and Mary Lou Trant, and my parents, Jane and Tony Urquhart, who provided help and guidance and also their homes for me to work in when I escaped from my own family life. I'm also indebted to my aunt-in-law, Adele Malo, for her eagle-eyed proofread.

I spoke with a long list of people for this book, and many of their names appear in these pages, but even when they don't, our conversations together inspired and informed this work. I can't list them because I would leave someone out and feel terrible, but their input was invaluable.

Thanks to Laurier University's Writer-in-Residence program for giving me an office and access to their library to get the ball rolling on this book.

Lastly, I'm grateful to my father, Tony Urquhart, for his generosity throughout this project, and throughout my artistic life. He was the first person to encourage me to tell stories.

©Andrew Trant

EMILY URQUHART is a National Magazine Award–
winning writer and has a doctorate in folklore from
Memorial University of Newfoundland. Her first book,
*Beyond the Pale: Folklore, Family, and the Mystery of Our
Hidden Genes*, was a *Maclean's* bestseller, a finalist for
the B.C. National Award for Canadian Non-Fiction,
and a *Globe and Mail* Best Book of 2015. Her freelance
writing has appeared in the *Toronto Star, The Walrus*
Magazine, *Longreads*, the *Rumpus*, and *Eighteen Bridges*,
among other publications. She is a nonfiction editor
for the *New Quarterly* and teaches creative nonfiction
at Wilfrid Laurier University. She lives in Kitchener,
Ontario, with her husband and their two children.